After thirteen successful novels, Joyce Stranger has produced her first non-fiction book; the story of her first pet, Kym, the remarkable Siamese cat whose exploits will amuse and delight her readers.

Mischievous, domineering, and destructive when crossed, he was endlessly in scrapes and frequently at the Vet's. His adventures are hair-raising and hilarious! He was also her loving, constant companion, riding on her shoulder at all times, and keeping up a flow of comments. A great conversationalist, he even managed to conduct a telephone call . . .

Joyce Stranger's family now includes a few more pets; two dogs, a puma, and two other Siamese cats. But there'll never be another pet like Kym. He was unique.

Also by JOYCE STRANGER

THE RUNNING FOXES
BREED OF GIANTS
REX
CASEY
RUSTY
CHIA THE WILD CAT
ZARA
WALK A LONELY ROAD
NEVER COUNT APPLES
NEVER TELL A SECRET
FLASH
ONE FOR SORROW
A DOG CALLED GELERT
A WALK IN THE DARK
KHAZAN
TWO'S COMPANY
LAKELAND VET

and published by CORGI BOOKS

Joyce Stranger

Kym

The True Story of a Siamese Cat

Text illustrations by William Geldart

CORGI BOOKS
A DIVISION OF TRANSWORLD PUBLISHERS LTD

KYM

A CORGI BOOK 0 552 10695 X

Originally published in Great Britain by
Michael Joseph Ltd.

PRINTING HISTORY

Michael Joseph edition published 1976
Corgi edition published 1978
Corgi edition reprinted 1980

This book is set in Baskerville 10/12 pt.

Corgi Books are published by Transworld Publishers Ltd.,
Century House, 61–63 Uxbridge Road, Ealing, London, W5 5SA

Made and printed in Great Britain by
Richard Clay (The Chaucer Press), Ltd., Bungay, Suffolk.

Dedicated to Kenneth and Andrew and the twins, who will say it wasn't a bit like that – and who didn't know half of it – and to Miss Collins, whose sole function in life, according to Kym, was to provide him with additional comfort and company, not to mention leaving food conveniently around for him to steal

Chapter 1

There have always been cats in my life as well as dogs. Many people are partisan, preferring one to the other. Numerous friends express surprise because I like both, fitting people into slots; cat people or dog people. They express even greater surprise when they visit my home now and find two cats and two dogs living amicably together. The cats often curl up against the dogs to keep warm. There is no need whatever to deprive oneself of one species because the house contains the other.

We have introduced a puppy into a house with an older cat; and a kitten into a home which already has a grown dog; we have had puppies and kittens at the same time. There is an initial settling down period but, handled properly, and introduced wisely, they do settle together, and often become great friends.

The first cat I remember really well was Nipper, who co-existed with our Airedale dog, Turk. Nipper must have had a fairly difficult life, as he came to us when my twin brother and sister were small and my younger sister was a baby. We all lugged him round constantly. I can't bear, now, to see a cat hoisted painfully by a little child, and insist that in our home the animals are treated with respect and not used as substitute toys. They usually endure without complaint, but should they rebel, unable to stand any more, the child may be badly hurt, and the animal will be blamed.

Once, when I was about eight, we dressed Nipper up in doll's clothes, and took him round the shops in my doll's pram. We were very careful to avoid our mother, as she would have been furious and stopped the game immediately, but we evaded her. She saw us go, thinking my big doll was in the pram.

In the very middle of Bexleyheath High Street, a dog pushed his nose under the hood. Nipper gave an eldritch yell and bolted, long clothes, bonnet, and all, into the street, where cars braked violently, tyres screaming. A tram was bearing down on both him and the dog.

There was pandemonium until a policeman fielded the cat, and brought him back to us. He was a very large and a very angry policeman, who shook me thoroughly, as I was the eldest of the three – the twins were only six. His anger taught me more than my mother's anger would have done; no one in those days questioned the authority of the police. Had my parents known of the incident they would both have said 'Serve you right', and added another punishment, such as no visit to the Zoo, or stopping our pocket money.

We took Nipper home and undressed him hastily. I am not sure that my mother ever did hear of this incident. I took very good care that it never happened to any of our cats when my own children were young.

Nipper was extremely large, very heavy, and coal black with green eyes. He had a number of unendearing habits, possibly provoked to them by us, as we loved him far too much, handled him far too much and he was rarely left in peace to get on with his own life. Someone always wanted to cuddle him.

One of his most annoying games was to lurk in the black shadows under the stairs, waiting for white-socked school-girl legs to run by. As they did, he leaped out, sank claws and teeth into our calves, and thoroughly enjoyed the resulting noise; leaping to the safety of the top of the hall cupboard, where he looked down with the greatest interest at whoever was yelling or bellowing at him.

He had another extremely maddening habit. We moved

8

house when he was about six years old. We went to live only a mile away from our original home, Lyndhurst, in Bexleyheath to a much bigger house called Broomwood. Nipper preferred our first home. Time after time during our first summer in the new house, I arrived back from school and was greeted by my mother.

'Nipper's gone back again. Will you go and get him, dear?'

Feeling most un-dear-like, I trudged across the dusty fields of cabbages along the footpath to Lyndhurst. I had to carry Nipper, protesting loudly and struggling vigorously, for over a mile.

Those cabbages never seemed to be harvested. Some years the price was too high for cutting them, and the profit too low, so they were left to rot and they stank. Other years they were soaked in continual rain and the crop was ruined and they rotted and they stank.

Black cats and the smell of rotting cabbages are irretrievably linked in my memory.

Nipper died at fifteen, and was succeeded by Sherry, a large and very beautiful tawny cat who spent most of his life lying in the sun.

Somewhere in the past there was also Snowball, so named because he was white. This was a misnomer, as he was born without the instinct to wash, and was the dirtiest cat I have ever seen.

I love cats. I love their grace and their elegance. I love their independence and their arrogance, and the way they lie and look at you, summing you up, surely to your detriment, with that unnerving, unwinking, appraising stare.

The war years were catless and dogless for me, except when I went home to my parents. I was away in hostel. I never passed a cat without stopping to make friends. With dogs I am more wary. One needs to know a dog before taking advantage; he may treat you as an intruder on his territory. However long one lives with dogs, it is never wise to go up to a strange one without reading his face and his tail, and parents who let children stroke my dogs without asking first if they may are fools. My dogs are safe approached the right way. Not all dogs are trustworthy by a long chalk. Many are unused to children, and alarmed by their noise and sudden uncontrolled movements. Many children are downright dangerous, unaware of animal needs.

After the war came marriage and babies. Twins, arriving when our elder son was only twenty months old, ensured there was no time for animals, however much I needed them. I knew I could not give a dog the exercise, training and companionship that he required. But I hankered for a cat.

I often saw Ming, a gorgeous animal, in the window of a local sweet shop. I made friends with him and coveted him. He was the most beautiful creature.

So that when my husband asked me, just before a birthday, what I wanted most in all the world, I answered without even stopping to think.

'A Siamese kitten.'

I did not expect to be provided with my dream. But Kenneth occasionally surprises me by producing the unexpected, choosing something rather exotic that I did not know I wanted.

So, six weeks later, feeling as if I had been given the crown jewels, I found myself sitting in our old car, holding a minute and bewildered scrap that was only big enough to balance on the palm of my hand. He was very beautiful and like all handsome creatures, he was aware of this throughout his long and crowded life.

His mask and ears were just beginning to colour. There was a hint of soot, as there was also on his paws and his kinked tail. The rest of him was a rich milky colour. His vivid blue eyes crossed when he was angry, and even at that age, reft from mother and litter mates, taken into the vast outside world at a mere nine weeks, he was not pining or pathetic.

He was furious.

He did not like us. He did not like the car. He intended that we should feel his resentment, and he yowled, long, loudly and determinedly, exclaiming at the arrangements we had made for him.

He hated us, he said. Very clearly and very plainly. He tried to scratch. I wrapped him tightly in an old jersey I had brought to keep him warm. It was a bitterly cold day. We were on the high bare moors, where he had been born in a very beautiful and luxurious home.

He hated the car. It made awful noises, and there were other noises as dinosaurian monsters hurtled towards us, far bigger than we were, obviously about to ram us and destroy us.

Even at that age he had a piercing voice and a habit of keeping up a running commentary in most expressive tones. He protested ever more loudly.

He was cold.

Rain lashed down the windscreen and obscured the bleak road. The few stunted, wintry trees were bare and twisted. The road wound among barren hills, where last year's bracken was a dismal dank rust which gave the moors an aura of despair. Years later, they were the scene of the Moors murders. I hate them now. They are haunted by horror and children's dying screams.

The car was old and had no heater. Kym huddled into the jersey, but it lacked comfort. He tried to warm himself, but there was no fur against him. Wool felt different. There was no contact of familiar bodies; nor was there his mother's swift tongue to reassure him. He was minute, among giants, who meant nothing to him, and who had stolen him from his home.

He escaped from the jersey and explored my lap, looking for a hiding place, wanting to be in the dark, which did not reveal so many new and frightening things to him.

He discovered a much better resting place.

This was also a jersey, but the jersey had a gap at the bottom that could be lifted by an exploratory paw. He could crawl under it, and under it was something that breathed as his mother had breathed, rhythmically, hypnotically. It didn't smell as nice as his mother. And it wasn't furry. But it was close and dark and comforting, and the hand above it smoothed his fur gently, reassuring him a little.

The protests died.

They were succeeded by a faint rusty sound we decided was a purr.

Thereafter sanctuary for Kym while he was small was a hurried scurry up inside my jersey. There he could lie against me, trembling, secure in the knowledge that no one and nothing could possibly get him there.

We reached home.

We now owned a small kitten, a huge piece of paper on which was written his pedigree, and a diet sheet, and had instructions to provide him with a tray of sand. The sand and the tray were bought on the way home. He dashed to it. His mother had taught him well. We put him on the tray, showing him how to scratch with his paw, so that he knew what it was for. He never once made a mistake, even when very ill. Kittens are much more endearing in that respect than puppies.

He sat with his back to us. He was always very modest.

Until that day pets had not been part of our children's lives. We had had stick insects, but they are not exactly appealing. Ours were rather stupid and invariably strangled themselves with their old skin when they moulted. There was nothing we could do about that. They were too fragile to handle.

We also, briefly, acquired a female newt as part of a swapping deal at school. She was named, outrageously,

Ivanhoe, after the TV serial at that time. Ivanhoe languished, in spite of a diet of daphne and ants' eggs, and one morning, convinced she would die on us, and hating having her captive in a goldfish bowl, I persuaded her owner to come with me and return her to the pond, where we hope she recovered. She simply sat on a stone, looking intensely miserable, all the time we had her.

Our boy and girl twins were seven years old when we bought Kym. They had come with us and helped to choose the kitten from a litter of five, a choice which had been easy, as Kym had been the one to approach us of his own free will and make friends, which he hadn't minded doing at all with his litter mates around him.

Our elder son was at a party. We decided we would surprise him, so he did not know we would have a new member of the family by the time he reached home. For that matter, I had not known until we arrived at our destination that afternoon.

The surprise was greater than we had intended as our son came in to find us all in the kitchen and the washing machine in pieces all over the floor. He was told that the reason for this was that somewhere inside, unhappily, in the dark, was a very small, very angry Siamese kitten that had made a bolt for the one safe hole when he saw his daunting new surroundings.

At that point the kitten spoke, confirming our story, which up to then had been thought to be rather an elaborate legpull.

We spent most of the evening in the kitchen, among the increasingly plentiful pieces of oily machinery. Kym had retreated right into the middle of the inside of the wretched machine. He had no desire to come out into the open and face the shrill, noisy, strange-smelling giants who now surrounded him. We had to block the hole and the back of the washing machine, and the hole behind the refrigerator, and the oven ventilator, and all the chimneys.

Some time later, after the children had gone to bed, he was extricated, a totally unrecognisable bedraggled scrap, shrieking in fury, hissing, scratching, and covered in oil. We did our best, but it was days before he was clean again.

He did not want food.

He did not want us.

He did not really want to be alone, but we could not provide him with his most urgent need, which was his old home, his mother and his litter brothers and sisters. I soothed him; I cuddled him; I petted him. I coaxed him to feed, just a few mouthfuls, giving him cornflakes in evaporated milk in my cupped hands. It is a messy procedure, but I always do it with new young animals, as the smell of the new owner inextricably mixed up with that of food helps a tiny bewildered creature recognise who is going to look after it and be substitute mum, and is the beginning of trust, which is essential for any human–animal relationship.

He recognised that I was the source of food. Having discovered that the natives, after all, were friendly, he promptly decided that my sole function was to nurse him. If we did not cuddle him, he climbed us, telling us off soundly as he did so. On one memorable occasion when we were in our caravan he climbed Kenneth, who, wearing thin summer pyjamas, was making an early morning cup of tea.

The resulting yell caused us all to be regarded with extreme suspicion for the rest of our stay on that site, as it was a little difficult to explain that it had been caused by the kitten using him as a tree. Kym obviously felt the pain we endured was just punishment for ignoring him. He was blissfully unaware that he might not be wanted; or that we had other things to do. We had been created for his benefit. He was capable of leaping on us without warning from anywhere in the house, be it the top of the wardrobe, the top of a door, or even the curtain pelmets. It hurt.

It also upset our small daughter, who decided, embarrassingly and annoyingly at this stage, that she hated cats, and ran screaming from him every time he jumped. This made him, being Kym, even more determined to jump on her. He could not see why she fled from him, so that I spent a great deal of time in those first few weeks with a small girl cuddled against me on one side, and a very much smaller indignant kitten curled on my lap, glaring at her, as I tried to reconcile the two of them. It needed as much work as the initial few days of a new puppy and kitten bought together.

Once she was converted she was his devoted servant, always ready to rescue him from his latest predicament.

His one aim in life, once he settled, was to brighten our days. There was always some piece of Kym mischief, or Kym misadventure to recount during an evening meal. He was extremely lively, extremely adventurous, and had enough curiosity for nineteen cats.

He also had double the number of cat lives and appeared to be anxious to lose every one of them.

He decided to get rid of his first life twenty-four hours after we acquired him. And being Kym, he did so as thoroughly as possible.

Chapter 2

We were novices at pedigree kitten buying. It did not occur to us that one needed to know a great deal before starting out; the breeding might be too close so that the resulting kits were highly nervous and had some major fault; the kittens might be unhealthy.

Had I known more we would not have bought Kym. Which would have been very wise, but it would have deprived us of years of pleasure, it would not have given me half the experience with animals that has led to many of my books, and most certainly we would have missed a great character.

I did the same thing with a dog years later. He too was a very bad buy. In spite of that, he has given me invaluable experience, and is a terrific character.

So perhaps it is not always wise to be sensible! But that does not absolve breeders from responsibility. Ailing animals are very expensive pets, and not always lucky enough to go to an owner who is prepared to take enough trouble to keep them alive. Many are put down because ill health or disability is a nuisance – and an unlooked-for expense in veterinary fees and special diets, which is an enormous waste of the breeder's time and money.

Kym would feed only from my hand; and he ate very little. I thought, for the first day, that this was because he was pining for his mother. On the second day he refused to eat at all. His voice, though still loud, had a fretful overtone. I examined his sand box closely when I went to empty it. What I saw took us both to the vet, although he was not due for his inoculations till the next week.

The vet examined him.

'Take him straight back', he said.

I looked at the kitten. He looked back at me. It was no use; the bond between us had been forged in those first few hours. I could not imagine what would happen to him if I did return him. Also he was a fierce little character, and I am not a giver-up.

I couldn't take him back.

'On your own head', the vet said. 'He has worms. Masses of them. His mouth is covered with ulcers.' He opened it, and showed me. The whole of Kym's tongue and palate was hidden by yellow encrusted swellings. 'He has a sore throat. He has cat 'flu. He can't possibly eat with that mouth. I can't do much for him. He needs vitamins and antibiotics. He'll die on you. There's far too much wrong with him.'

He was not going to die on me.

And if I took him back to someone who had let him get into that condition before selling him, he undoubtedly would die, as they hadn't the knowledge to save his life. I hadn't much knowledge, but I obey instructions whether given by vet or doctor, feeling I have paid for advice and it's insane not to take it. And I would obey the instructions this vet gave me to the letter.

Kym was lying on the table, looking very small, very sick and very pathetic. His beautiful eyes were obscured by their third membrane, which the vet told me was a sure sign of worms; his coat had not recovered from the oil in the washing machine; his nose was running, and he was dribbling so much that his throat was soaked with saliva.

I held him for that first injection.

Enraged, he yelled. He had a pretty considerable voice.

His small paw struck angrily at the man who had inflicted such indignity on him. It looked like Tom Thumb defying a giant.

'Well, he seems to have some life in him', the vet

observed, but I knew from his expression that he did not think I would win.

I accept defeat with an old animal at the end of its life, when it is cruel and selfish to prolong pain, but I will not accept defeat with a young creature. I was going to fight. Every inch of the way, and the kitten was going to fight with me.

By the next day he was a very sick little cat. He had to have daily injections, and I knew every time I saw the vet's expression that he considered me a fool, throwing my money away on a useless cause. Which only made me more determined.

Kym was equally determined. He might be ill; he might feel awful, but there was one thing certain, and that was that as his mother wasn't here to comfort him, I had to do instead. No matter how he felt, he clawed his way up to me to lie in my lap, small head almost limp and lifeless against my hands, eyes staring into the fire at nothing.

Friends told one another it was pointless calling as I had become addicted to a kitten. As I was giving him five drops of glucose and water every fifteen minutes from an eye dropper I had bought from the chemist, I wasn't very attentive to conversation. My mind was on other things.

I rapidly became expert with the dropper.

While I was writing, Kym lay in my lap. While I was busy about the house, he lay in a small cardboard box, lined with a blanket under which was a hot water bottle. As he wailed if I were not near him, I carried it with me, and he watched me make beds, and work around the house generally. I was determined he would not give up hope; once he himself determined to die, nothing I could do would stop him. He had to feel he was wanted. It wasn't easy, as I was strange to him, and during those first days there were moments when even I was sure I was going to lose. The vet never doubted it. He told me not to waste any more money, and to accept the inevitable.

19

My life revolved around glucose, water and the eye dropper.

A few drops, every quarter of an hour, fighting to keep him alive. Whatever happened now, he was not going to die on me, and every new day was an achievement. The children were upset, and I had rashly promised them that Kym wouldn't die. They knew promises were always kept.

Kym would live.

His feeble greeting each morning was reassurance to me that the struggle was not yet over.

At that time our lives were brightened every Wednesday and Friday by the visit of our greengrocer, Tom, who owned a horse and cart. He loathed lorries, and always said that when his horse died, he would die too. He only survived Prince by a very few months when at last the old horse went.

Tom was a countryman. His brother was a gamekeeper in Cumberland. Tom's visits to me, marked by cups of tea in summer and soup in winter, were always long talks on the habits of wild animals. He had hunted foxes; two men with guns and dogs, trying to keep the population from running riot. Two men on one hill on one Saturday killed seventy foxes, and there were more left to run. A vixen can have fifteen in a litter; if all survive, they will die of starvation anyway.

When Tom's horse had colic, Tom paid a boy to trot the horse around, while he drew the cart. He knew about animals; knew about horses, dogs and cats; knew many ways of fattening a pig, and had lived for a long time in the country himself. Goodness knows how he came to be a suburban greengrocer. He was a shy man, but he never could resist talking about country matters, or about racing, as he knew a great deal about both the breeding of racehorses and their form. Though I learned through him that a lot of horses don't run according to their form!

There had never been a small animal in our house. Tom

20

laughed at our stick insects and recommended returning Ivanhoe to the pond. He now came in to get warm, and bent down to look at Kym, in his box by the fire, an old-fashioned kitchen stove with an oven beside it, and a vast metal guard to ensure safety.

'What's that? A weasel?'

'That' certainly didn't look much like a kitten. Kym was lying on his side, eyes closed, ribs barely moving. It was one of his worst days. I kept cleaning his nose and mouth, but the dribbling and discharge was continuous and he looked terrible. Tom turned him over.

'He's half dead', he said. 'You'll never rear that. Better take it to the vet now. You're wasting your time.'

People are always telling me what I can't do. *You'll* never write a book. *You'll* never learn to drive. *You'll* never train a dog.

Little do they know. I'll show them.

'Want to bet?' I asked Tom, knowing his main weakness.

He took me on at once, but I would have liked to hedge that bet, as just for once I wasn't at all sure I was going to win it.

Luckily Kym had a tough ancestry. The day came when I arrived proudly at the vet with a clear-eyed kitten that had eaten solid food for the first time, and looked as if he would survive. By the end of the week he had lustrous fur, was racing round the house, and the vet had changed his opinion of me. He had thought me a fool. Now he knew I wasn't.

Tom paid his five shillings. We were neither of us reckless gamblers.

And then the fun began.

Kym now knew he was *my* cat. I had nursed him, cuddled him and forced food into him. I had been so determined that I had given him the will to live. I had never left him by day and had come down several times to feed and dose him each night. I had carried him upstairs when I went up, and he had never been separated from me while I was busy.

So he was now my shadow, as devoted as any dog. He followed me everywhere, yelling at the top of his voice if I dared to shut a door on him and leave him outside.

I thought it time to show him the garden. The days were warmer, and the earth box could be abandoned. But Kym hated the outside. He was very small, and sat there, complaining, because the wind shook the giant trees, and sobbed invisibly in their branches, so that they rose and swept across the sky, daunting him.

He hated the unseen fingers that ruffled his fur.

He raced to me, swarmed up me, sat on my shoulder, peered into my face, his eyes crossed, his voice excited, apparently declaiming in detail in a long monologue everything that had happened to him. It was so funny that I sometimes laughed, hurting his feelings beyond measure. He loathed being laughed at.

I don't like humanising animals, but they undoubtedly communicate, and you can learn a lot of their language. My present Alsatian has a special dance that she performs when her water bowl is empty. Kym had his means of communicating. He sat and willed the refrigerator or the pantry doors to open; he would rattle at the back door, yowling till I opened it; he sat in sink or bath, trying to get his tongue up the tap, if his water bowl were empty; and in the caravan he soon learned to tap the chain that kept the lids of the water carriers from getting lost. Each gesture had its own cry with it, so that he changed tones when he wanted different things.

His telling-me-about-the-world voice was extremely expressive, as if he were exclaiming and underlining, declaiming and commenting. In a strange place he used to reduce all of us to laughter as we could trace his progress by his voice, making sounds of astonishment, or delight, or giving a sudden yell for help as something enormous appeared on his horizon, which was always much more limited than ours.

He walked in a jungle when he was in long grass; in summer a tropical jungle, high above his head. Lie down at his level and the ground was humid, the air fetid. He learned to jump to a branch and sit where he could breathe more easily, out of the private forest that only the small beasts know.

Whenever anything bothered Kym, he climbed me. This was so painful that I developed an early warning system, listening for the anguished yowl that announced his coming. He was so very small. It might mean that there was an enormous nasty dog looking at him through the fence, vast tongue slavering as he panted hopefully, or a giant cat had invaded our territory, threatening him, or worse, chasing him.

None of the local established cats liked our Siamese. In his early days he was chivvied mercilessly. I sometimes thought they might have killed him if they had caught up with him, but luckily he could run very fast.

Meanwhile the garden was still unexplored territory and the earth box dominated both our lives. I kept trying to make him accept the outside. But he would only venture a few steps, crouched belly low against the ground, ears pricked, eyes wild, obviously a soldier going into enemy territory, needing all his senses alert. The least sound sent him scurrying to me, and the only way to prevent needle-like claws gripping my skin, leaving innumerable pinpricks in a traverse that showed where he had climbed, was to be ready for him, to grab him fast, and to sit him on my shoulder.

He was also so lethal to stockings that I rarely wore a skirt at all. I live in slacks. It's cheaper with cats and dogs, and much more comfortable. Even with slacks, Kym's claws could still penetrate.

Neighbours, friends and tradesmen became resigned to

seeing me open the front door with a small vociferous kitten sitting, like a witch's familiar, face against mine, doing his best to drown our conversation. He was even more successful in blotting out telephone calls. He hated the telephone. It was obviously ridiculous to him to see me talking away to that piece of plastic, with nobody there but him. Sure I could only be talking to him, he tried to make me look less absurd by answering everything I said before my caller could.

On one memorable occasion my husband 'phoned, asking me for the number of his passport as he was due to go on a trip abroad. I went to look, and left Kym sitting on the window sill beside the 'phone. At the other end of the line, Kenneth made some comment to his secretary. Kym recognised the voice, stuck an experimental paw into the receiver, bent his head and said 'Waugh' so clearly that my husband answered 'Hallo, fool'. Kym replied and they carried on a hilarious conversation until I came back, with me able to hear both sides. I only hoped his secretary had left the office. It may sound daft to talk to a cat on the telephone, but everyone who knew Kym had to admit that he was that sort of cat.

Kim and I soon started a battle of wills. Our first clash came one lovely sunny day when I was planting our new rockery with heathers. As fast as I put a plant in, Kym took it out and carried it in a triumphal march round the lawn. I captured him, replanted, and finally lost my temper and gave him a very hard tap across the paws.

He hissed at me and scratched, at which point I became mother cat and gave him a cuff on the ears. He recognised discipline at once. No mother animal allows her young to take liberties, and he knew now that I was boss. He came to my lap and curled up and licked my hand, and purred, a very sorry kitten. The rest of the heathers went in without trouble.

This did not always work.

He was the most persistent cat I have ever known, even for a Siamese. I now have two others, but they are nothing like as wilful as Kym. If I ignored him he leaned forward and tried to insert his paw into my mouth, presumably imagining that this would make me speak. Open mouths uttered words, and words meant a great deal to that particular cat. He loved them. He even understood some of them, like food, and garden, and come, but he was a very long time indeed learning to respect the one tiny word that is important to all animals, whether human or otherwise: *No!*

Chapter 3

Kym learned the art of blackmail very early. If I denied him my lap, because I was busy, or denied him food, because it was not yet time, he went to attack what he obviously felt was our most cherished possession: our big armchair, which has a cover on it that is quite impossible for a small cat not to sharpen his claws on. The instant NO acknowledging that he had been noticed was all he wanted. Just attention. Sometimes he would sit there, paw raised, watching me, while I pretended not to see. He didn't attempt to scratch until I looked at him. At once he put his paw in position, attracting a yell of 'No. Bad cat. No.'

At this point, having gained his objective, he moved to the windowsill, a very smug expression on his face. There he washed, ostentatiously, his attitude saying 'I never wanted to do it anyway.'

We never did cure him of using the carpet on the bottom stair as a scratching post. He had scratching blocks and scratching trees, but the bottom stair, when we were out, was a place where he could lie on his side, push with his hind paws and rake with his front paws. A frayed stair carpet on that bottom step was a major feature of the house while Kym was alive. We replaced it several times, but we never cured him. My present cats are angelic about scratching, always using the pads, and we have respectable carpets.

He also tore wallpaper, and if I punished him, by shaking and scolding, he rushed to the mantelpiece, leaped up, and quite deliberately pushed my ornaments onto the hearth, watching in delight as they broke. He looked up gleefully, awaiting my reaction. He moved so fast that I never forestalled him and in the end we replaced all our ornaments with wooden ones that don't break when dropped. We still have them. I never dust them without being reminded of Kym, sitting on the mantelpiece, watching them fall. We never knew when he would indulge himself and try and smash my possessions, apparently to pay me out for thwarting him in some piece of wickedness he had just invented.

It was impossible to ignore him. If I shut him out of a room I soon discovered I couldn't stand the din he made, as he would not be quiet until I opened the door and let him in. He had an enormous voice which made a neighbour once quote to me a saying she had heard, that an ordinary cat will wake its owner, but a Siamese will wake the dead. She didn't like Siamese cats at all.

Nor could I leave him grounded, as even when he was fully grown, and weighed fourteen pounds, he would climb me, or leap me, almost knocking me backwards if he jumped while I was moving about and got his distance wrong.

He rode me while I peeled potatoes, commenting the whole time. He rode me while I made the beds. He sat on my shoulder, bellowing into my ear, varying his conversation with a swift lick that tickled horribly and always took me by surprise. He loved washing me and when he had finished his own toilet, which was meticulous and performed nightly in my lap around nine o'clock, he would wash both my hands and any part of my arms that were not covered, and then put a paw on my hand and laugh at me. This meant it was time to wash his tail, which I held for him as it had a habit of twitching out of his reach and annoying him. It was a particularly uncontrollable tail, it seemed, and did not always do what he wanted it to do.

He loved me to try and catch it so that he could twitch it away from me.

Kym's life outside the house was one long adventure. I often felt that he had the same tendencies as my small sons, who delighted to tell me how narrowly they had escaped death under the wheels of cars, bicycles, lorries, or by not falling out of the tallest tree in the world, which happened, very conveniently, to be on the local playground, and a great temptation to adventurous children.

Kym's life obviously seemed to him just like that, as there were so many hazards. There was the road, which he learned to dash across at breakneck speed. I often wished he would confine himself to our back garden, but behind the houses on the other side there were fields, and there was a multitude of small animals.

There is an alley way between the houses opposite, ending in a stile. I can still see the remains of the fields as I write, but a new housing estate is obliterating our last wild space. Few people realised how wild those scanty acres were. I did not myself until I took to hunting for Kym in the long grass, where the cattle grazed.

There he found a country of his own; cuckoo flowers bloomed profusely in spring, and small mice hid as they heard his footsteps. Magpies nested in the tall tree, and yacked when they heard him coming. He watched all swift movement in the grasses. A weasel would appear, briefly, racing for cover, and vanish. Within moments the cat was busy with another clump of grass in which a mouse quivered. Not for long. Kym was a great mouser though he rarely killed them. He brought them home, proudly, and I took them from him, praised him, took him in, fed him, and returned the mouse to the field, hoping it would find its own way home. These were field mice, and no threat to us.

There were rabbits, which often lolloped down the road in the early morning, before the speeding cars arrived to scare them away. They sat in our garden.

Sometimes, when the grass was high in next door's back patch where their English setters roamed, the long ripe grass-seed ears hung invitingly over my fence. I would hear a sharp chik chik of anger from the cat, sitting in the window, eyes glaring, chattering his teeth in fury, as the rabbits stood on hind legs and pulled down the succulent seeds to eat. They were surprisingly long when they stood erect and neither Kym nor I moved until they had finished, though we stood there for different reasons.

Once they had gone I let him out, and he paced the lawn, sniffing at the ground where they had passed, plainly learning all about them.

Next door's tawny cat, Marmaduke, was a great rabbiter, and I thought Kym might prove the same. Kym's first real outdoor encounter with a wild rabbit occurred when he was small. We had a full grown buck arrive in the garden and crouch under the plum tree, enjoying the shade. Kym had just gone outside. He was playing with a leaf, twisting and turning, whirling and twirling, in the elfin dance that always fascinated me so much that I forgot what I was doing and watched him enjoying his life as only a small child or an animal can, absorbed in the present, with no thought of the future and only random memories of the past.

He saw the rabbit just as the old buck saw him. He was a magnificent buck, full grown and very large. He sat up, his back to the cat, watching it over one shoulder with curious eyes. He had certainly never seen a Siamese cat before as at that time Kym was the only one in the district. He was now half grown, with long black paws, long black tail, a black mask, and crossed blue eyes that annoyed our doctor, who wanted the squint corrected. Those eyes were, many years later, to lead me to one of the oddest encounters of my life.

Kym saw the rabbit and sat, not sure what to make of this enormous beast. Not sure even if it were a rabbit, as those that came to nibble the grass ears were much smaller – probably this year's babies, half grown. This was Dad, immense, majestic, a rabbit to end all rabbits.

Dad knew about cats. He continued to look, ready to bound away if there was any threat from the much smaller animal at the other end of the lawn. Kym turned his back, and sat, apparently thinking. He washed one hind paw, very carefully, from end to end, sticking it at an angle into the air, examining it meticulously.

He peeped over his shoulder.

Rabbit, plainly mystified, was peeping over *his* shoulder.

Kym nibbled hastily at an itch, and swished his tail. Perhaps if he pretended Rabbit wasn't there, it would go away. It was his garden, after all. Rabbit turned his back again and gazed into space.

Kym washed the other leg.

Very slowly, as if unable to resist the temptation, he turned his head again, only to find that Rabbit had turned his head. Mesmerised, they stared at one another.

By now I had totally forgotten about housework, and had poured a cold drink and was sitting on the windowsill to watch the outcome. Both animals continued to peer at one another at intervals for almost forty minutes. Neither moved from the spot on which he was firmly and safely anchored. It seemed as if this could go on all day. I was just reluctantly concluding that I really had better get on with my own affairs when both animals, as if given a signal, loped very slowly away in opposite directions.

Rabbit hopped in long slow bounds. Kym sneaked along, belly almost on the ground, until he came round the corner of the house, when he exploded into a run, raced in through the door, jumped to the table and then to my shoulder and launched into a long complicated involved monologue about what had been going on and how he had seen this enormous animal and it had sat there and had looked at him.

Try as I would, it was impossible not to feel he was giving a most explicit account of the goings-on out on the lawn. His voice rose and fell, soft, then loud, then exclamatory, until I was so helpless with laughter that he leaped off my shoulder on to the windowsill and sat there, back to me, his tail lashing to and fro, absolutely furious with me because I had dared to laugh at him.

He found other things in the fields. There was a hare, and leverets, though luckily he never caught one. They were always well hidden but if I sat and watched the mother, I could usually see just where she had put her babies. They were always far apart. Then if one nest was raided, the others survived. The bound she made sideways off the nests was incredible, a vast leap which killed her scent, and foiled any dogs tracking her. Years later she found her way into *The Hare at Dark Hollow*, and on to *Jackanory*.

There were moles and shrews and voles. There were birds. Kym loved bringing me presents. I became used to taking them from him and freeing any that were unharmed. He rarely did kill his prey, except for the moles, which were invariably dead. Perhaps they fought him; or perhaps he found them when they were already dying, due to the attentions of a mole-catcher.

I always put Kym indoors before freeing his catch. He invariably went out an hour later to see if it was there, where he had left it. It never was. Those animals he did kill I found were almost always maimed; and I suspected the others were ill. He killed a one-legged blackbird, that was starvation thin; and a thrush which had a giant growth pushing the two parts of its beak wide open so that it could not have been able to feed for days. Other animals often had old injuries on them, so that I feel that cats, like other predators, cull, taking out the sickly creatures from the breeding cycle and improving the stock. For all that I dislike cat habits in that respect, one learns to live with it. It is a natural thing. If he caught a bird that was unharmed, I always put it high on our bird table, surrounded by a large quantity of wild birdfood. The presence of the other birds, coming for food, seemed to be a splendid antidote for shock. The bird invariably fed after about thirty minutes and then flew away.

The wise birds were never caught, as they soon knew our cat's progress. I used to say to friends who had called for coffee (after lunch, as the morning is always my working time at my typewriter), 'Just a minute. Cat's coming', and I would go out of the room and let him in.

It was only when one of my closer friends got desperate and revealed that she and everyone else I knew regarded this as an uncanny and rather peculiar party trick, on a par with my witchlike habit of wearing Kym on my shoulder, that I realised how few people actually are aware of what is going on around them.

It was so obvious that I just couldn't see why they didn't know too.

Yet when I tried to explain I only added to their mystification.

The birds had told me.

The *birds*?

Birds are wonderful guardians for all wild things. I would hear those first angry notes of 'cat, cat, cat' in the far distance, across the fields. Kym had been hunting.

Then the calls came nearer. The magpies chickered in the big birch tree halfway down the twelve acre field; the thrushes that nested in the thorn hedge passed on the call; the robin added his sharp little note of warning, as Kym approached the garden shed where Robin and his mate hid their babies; and then came the yells from the thrushes in the laurel bush in the front garden opposite our own house.

Now my birds were yelling loud and furious, deafening me with their sounds. They were telling me, as plain as if they were speaking in my own language, that Kym had come round the corner of the house opposite, was in full view crossing the road, was coming up my garden path, was waiting by the front door.

It couldn't be plainer.

Whenever he appeared, I came out and picked him up and took him in. If he were stalking birds on the lawn, I picked him up even more quickly. Within a very few weeks of the start of Kym's hunting life, cat and I were identified as one by the birds. If I appeared, Kym was almost certain to come too, either following me from the house, or racing to me from somewhere in the garden.

The warnings started, in time, as soon as I appeared, even if the cat were nowhere near. We were inseparable and I was obviously equally dangerous. In the same way a falconer, hunting often in the same place, finds the birds will shout, not when the hawk appears, but when the van he is travelling the bird inside comes into view. It is soon useless hunting there; all the birds have vanished before the hawk is on his fist.

Our birds stayed put, so long as the cat did not appear in the tree.

They never yell now, as my two blue point Siamese, Chia and Casey, exercise in a cage; a very large pen made for the dogs. I can't face the troubles we had with Kym with two of them. The birds ignore the dogs. I am no longer a threat, and no bird shouts at me.

Once Kym was inside he amused my guests by pacing the floor, eyes crossed, tail swishing, declaiming loudly with all the assurance of a born actor. Having informed us all of his adventures, he then jumped to my lap, and, with a deep sigh of content, turned himself around until he was comfortable, and proceeded to bath, washing delicately, inspecting each paw, and nibbling between the pads. Exhausted, he curled up to sleep, first putting his paw firmly on my hand to make sure I couldn't knit. He hated knitting.

In the end, after nightly battles during which he pulled the wool off the needles, or teased at them until I dropped a stitch, I gave in, and became an ardent patron of St Michael instead. I never had liked knitting, but my mother and my mother-in-law both made me feel so guilty if I didn't indulge in this housewifely chore that I did try. My children sighed as they pulled on yet another garment that appeared to have been put together haphazardly, and rejoiced when I gave up.

I dressmade for a couple of years longer, until my daughter went to a party and came home and said rather wistfully, 'Can I have a proper dress from a shop before I go to another party?'

Thankfully I gave that up too. I could now write with an easy conscience. Kym approved of that as he could curl in my lap, or lie beside the typewriter, or sit in the cupboard and occasionally regale me with his latest bit of hot cat news.

By the time he was eight months old he was much more independent. But he still needed protection from Dusky, next door.

Dusky was an immense Persian who had regarded my garden as his for some years. He was a very dignified cat, and he was appalled when I imported a small screeching demon that didn't look like a proper cat, didn't sound like a proper cat, and seemingly didn't even smell like a proper cat. It was very easy for Dusky to be bold as he was twenty times the size of my kitten, and could see him off in seconds by fluffing his fur up to immense size, which was really tremendous as he had a very long coat. He then emitted an ear-splitting yowl.

What with Dusky howling and Kym yelling that Dusky was after him again and please come quick, it was very difficult to ignore the cats. Occasionally my kitten exploded into the kitchen through the open window instead of the door, landing on the kitchen table. Once I was making pastry and Kym landed in the bowl in a flurry of flour that didn't please either of us.

Even worse than Dusky was Beagle. This area has been dominated for a great many years by a succession of wandering beagles, probably all belonging to the same family, though I have never been quite sure of that. Each is allowed to wander as he chooses, let out in the morning to wreak mayhem, treeing cats, chasing other dogs, importuning in-season bitches, trespassing in gardens where they eat the birds' food, and leaving unpleasant mementos on lawn or doorstep.

One of the least endearing habits they have is to chase cats. After all, they are bred for hunting, and hunt they will. The beagle that was contemporary with Kym chased little girls when he ran out of cats. But most of all he liked to make a detour that included our garden, so that he could chase Kym. No fence deterred him. He could climb over, or barge through, being a hefty little dog, and make a new gap. I like most dogs, but I grew to detest Beagle, all of them. No one has ever taught them NO.

Kym usually found a clear space to run home, but not always. He ran to trees. He was once marooned at the top of a telegraph pole. That was quite a morning, as there were men working on the next pole and they tried, very kindly, to get my kitten down.

He removed himself to the very tip of the pole and screamed.

'Being stolen!'

I ran out, armed with a plateful of fish.

'Don't touch that, it's vicious', said a large man, sucking a long scratch on his hand.

I rattled the plate against the pole. Kym slipped down, sliding most of the way, emitting an agitated wail rather like a miniature air-raid siren. He landed on my shoulder where he became a melting adoring thank-you-for-rescuing-me I-do-love-you purring cat, much to the men's amazement.

'He was frightened', I explained with as much dignity as

was possible with a plate of coley in one hand and a kitten rolling against my face, balanced on my shoulder, supported by the other hand.

The men were speechless as we walked away, Kym declaiming loudly, like a newsboy yelling Read All About It.

I never liked leaving Kym when I was out during the day. Something always went wrong. Once I came home and found him lying miserably in the lavender bush, with a strip of fur and skin about six inches long and an inch and a half wide missing from between his shoulders. It was an injury that baffled me, and baffled our vet. It could have been done by a dog, but it was too regular. I suspected a vandal for years, until I happened to mention it to another veterinary friend. He had seen a similar injury on a cat that had been run over by a car; something under the car had caught it on the back, and had made the same mark.

Apart from possible injuries, if I was going to the shops and Kym was in the garden he had his own way of ensuring that I didn't go it alone. A small shape would suddenly appear from the last house in the road that led to the village, and greet me with fervour. He had run through the gardens, invisible to me. He would then jump to my shoulder, to ride with me the rest of the way.

This was far from convenient, so that I had to go home, put Kym indoors and start out again. Neighbours who didn't know me must have thought me insane. But there is never any choice with a Siamese. If he wanted to ride my shoulder, he rode my shoulder. My present little male, Casey, won't be picked up unless he chooses, but Chia is a shoulder rider. She too gives me no choice.

I could argue with Kym all I liked. But back he came.

I had to devise a way to get him in, or I wasted a great deal of time hunting for him, looking under bushes and up trees and calling, which had no effect whatever, as if he didn't want to come, he didn't come.

I found out how to get him in by accident. He had a very mysterious habit of appearing the second I put food on his plate. I realised after much puzzling that it was an enamel plate and his quick ears caught the sound of fork or knife on metal.

Even then it didn't dawn on me that I could use this to advantage. One day I was beating eggs (for a cake) in a metal bowl. Kym appeared, eager, positive I had summoned him for food, and was so annoyed to find he was wrong that he tried to steal the eggs. I gave him a little taste of fish, and sent him out again, not realising just why he had come in.

I started beating the eggs again and this time he came in even quicker, quite sure I had made a mistake and I really was making his dinner.

Thereafter whenever we wanted Kym we beat a fork against a plate. The sound was enough to bring him at top speed, legs going so fast that they seemed to cross over as he ran. It was the only time he ever lost his dignity. Many distant neighbours must have wondered at the frequent tocsin sounds from our garden, and so must those on caravan sites who were too far away to see the cat coming, summoned like the genie of the lamp by our din.

I often fed him tiny meals several times a day as it was more convenient to know he was safely shut indoors. This was particularly so when he grew up, since he made up for all that he had been made to suffer as a kitten by becoming Emperor of the road, insisting it was all his territory and beating up the neighbourhood cats, a habit that didn't really endear him to anyone, even though their pets had made his life a minor hell when he was small.

Kym's only defence as a kitten was to emit a fearsome yell, a weird screech that was enough to appal some visiting cat that thought he had an easy victim.

I soon discovered there is as much myth about the Siamese cat as there is about having babies. I was told they are exceptionally delicate (cats, not babies; they suffer from other peculiarities known to all the Jonahs who visit expectant mothers). The fragile Siamese rarely survives its first few weeks, so of course as soon as Kym was ill, everybody told me so. It is a delicate eater, only able to stomach things like chicken, turbot, halibut, and possibly steamed plaice.

If it should survive its youth, it is fierce, untamable, likely to scratch out the children's eyes, to ruin the furniture and to rip the curtains into shreds. It also makes an unpleasant, raucous, non-stop noise.

I love the noise. I was also sure I could tame a kitten. It is all a matter of training; some things you can teach a cat, but few people do try and train them. All my cats understand NO. And that has multiple uses. Chia and Casey also understand and respect OUT, used when they trespass in the pantry, or the room with our respectable chairs.

Kym survived his first illness.

He did make a noise, but he was extremely gentle, in spite of the apparent ferocity of his comments. We had daily games, most of which he invented. One of his favourites was to help make the beds. This meant bed-making took about five times as long as usual. The routine was unvarying. All animals and most humans love routine as it makes for order in a very disorderly world.

The games began with Kym sitting on the bed, eyes half closed, looking wicked, mumbling at me in an odd cross between a yowl and a purr, until I realised what he wanted and pushed my fist hard against his forehead. Back went his ears and he thrust his head hard against me. Just as I was beginning to tire of this part of the game, he rolled over, seized my fist in his mouth and covered it in tiny love nibbles, kicking against me with his hind legs, claws sheathed.

He held my arms firmly in his front paws, which were velvet soft against my skin. At first, while he was small, he sometimes became over-excited, and yelled in sudden frenzy and leaped clear. As he grew older he learned to control that, and the game ended with him nestled against me, crooning, delighting in contact, so that he rubbed his furry face against my cheek.

Only then could the bed-making proceed. Often I had to open up the blankets again, as he would either leap in from the opposite side of the bed and lie flat against the bed foot, or he would slip inside unseen and apparently vanish so that I searched the house for him until I saw that telltale hump, warm under the blankets, enjoying hiding while I sought.

Sometimes he merely leaped up and did a dervish dance, racing frenziedly round the bed, under the blanket, trying to catch my hand and pounce on it as I tucked in the bedding. I loathe bed-making, but Kym certainly livened up the process, and it usually ended in a wild romp as he chased off, and came back again to tease at anything I happened to hold in my hand.

He listened very anxiously for us to get up. He slept in the kitchen which was very warm, as we had an all-night fire there. His box was in the corner of the room, with an earth box against emergencies under the table. We never did know if he had emptied himself during the evening, and it seems to me absurd to trust to luck and then complain. The box is easy to clean and cats respect it. Kym never did make a mess anywhere in the house.

One day he was sick in the hall and this obviously worried him. I was having a bath. He came rushing upstairs, and stood on his hind legs and tried to hook me out of the water. At last, realising he had something urgent to communicate and maybe needed to go outside, I went down, to be shown the mess on the floor. Once it was cleaned up he relaxed; I had done my duty and could go back and finish my bath, while he went to sleep again. He had been eating grass, and I had brought him in before he had had time to get rid of it. Animals seem to use this as a cleansing habit.

It's not a sign of diet deficiency or ill health. It may get rid of worms in wild animals.

Kym never bit, but he would not allow anyone to pick him up unless he chose. He perched high above them, watching them suspiciously, until he was sure they were friendly. My friends he always honoured by sitting on their laps, a pleasure not appreciated by non-cat-lovers, but Kym was blithely unaware of that.

Mary, who lives across the road, is allergic to cats. For some reason best known to Kym it was always her doorstep he chose to sun himself on, and her garden he used as a direct route to the field beyond. He had several adventures in it owing to his insistence in using it as a right of way.

On one occasion black cotton was strung to keep the birds off the crocuses, which were planted thickly, in large beautiful clumps, on either side of a small flight of stone steps that led down to the lawn. Black cotton must be invisible to cats, as Kym tripped, somersaulted in a totally undignified way, and landed on the grass, where he sat, washing furiously, to cover his embarrassment.

That did not cure him of using the garden. Other cats also made it their main path to the field, so that one day Mary met me and said, 'Have you seen a bald ginger cat anywhere? Kym fought him in my garden. Do come and look.'

It was impossible to believe any cat could have lost so much fur and not be bald, but when I looked somewhat anxiously at the various gingers round us, they all seemed intact. Kym had a bite on his shoulder. Within a few days this proved to be the first of the many abscesses that were to lead us to beat out a path to the vet's, and earn Kym the nickname of Battling Billy. We were soon only too well known, as those abscesses invariably needed lancing and injections of antibiotic to clear them up. Somehow Kym always got bitten in the sort of place that is impossible to see until it does go wrong and however carefully I examined him after a fight, I never could find anything other than scratches at first.

I sometimes suspected Kym of a misplaced sense of humour as often after a fight that had sounded like the encounter of two spitting demons, yelling loudly enough to wake the dead, I would discover he had gone to earth either in Mary's garden (apparently bent on making her change her mind about cats, though he was going about it in quite the wrong way) or else somewhere in the road, not coming when he was called, staying away so long we decided that this was the end; he had fought to the death; or he had been run over; or he had been stolen. That is another thing that happens to Siamese cats, according to one's informers, though I suspect anyone trying to steal Kym would have had an exceptionally unpleasant few hours, and never have been able to stand him afterwards, as he rarely stopped 'talking'.

Just as we had given up all hope of ever seeing him again, he would appear with a wicked look in his eyes, greeting us fervently, surprised that we had been looking for him at all.

His favourite trick was to climb our apple tree, at the far end of the garden. There he would sit, pathetic, forlorn, *stuck*. Getting up was fine, his voice seemed to be telling us, but coming down was different. He sounded as if he were chiding us for being too slow, leaving him up there when he wanted to be down with us.

The children always rushed to his rescue when they were home, climbing the tree, handing him down gently to me, where he cuddled on my shoulder, so grateful to be safe again.

Then one day, after he had been rescued twice, the children all went out to tea. Strangely, he rarely climbed the tree when I was alone. I was talking on the telephone when I heard the anguished yowls and knew he was marooned again. There was nothing I could do about it at that moment.

I rang off, and rather unnervingly, the cries stopped. I wondered if he had fallen and, uncatlike, had damaged himself. I couldn't imagine any other reason for the silence as normally he yelled until someone came.

I went out into the garden.

There, swiftly, competently, as if he had done it a hundred times, as he probably had, was my little cat, coming down the apple tree. He saw me and froze, two inches from the ground, and began to shout again. I'm stuck, I'm stuck, I'm stuck.

I laughed so much that he was furious. He jumped the last inches and stalked indoors and sat for the whole evening with his back to me, his tail swishing angrily at intervals. By bedtime he had forgiven me and was once more purring on my lap, helping me read.

This was a common and not very useful exercise, as his idea of help was to flip the pages back as I turned them over, sure that there was a much better way of dealing with yet another peculiar human activity. It took my attention away from him and annoyed him nearly as much as the telephone. My dogs peer with great interest at my book and sniff it before turning away in disgust. I often wonder what they make of human doings. An animal lives its life in an aura of constant and bewildering mystery conforming to rules it can never understand. It must feel as we would if isolated in a foreign country with unfamiliar etiquette and no interpreter, having to conform because we would be punished if we didn't.

Letter writing was even worse than reading books, from Kym's point of view, but it did hold more interesting possibilities. Pens could be played with. They could be carried away and hidden. They could be tapped to make interesting squiggles across the page. This was particularly rewarding as it invariably made me say something to him. Never mind that the something was said in anger. He wasn't being ignored. I knew he was there and had noticed him.

Pens could also be stalked and pounced at.

Papers, to Kym, were wonderful. They rustled. Christmas was the most exciting time in his life, when everyone had papers round them; tissues and golden paper that crinkled, and ribbons to tease, as well as baubles to knock off the Christmas tree. But failing Christmas every day, he settled for the newspaper.

That too rustled. It could be jumped at, when it tore with a satisfying rip and an equally satisfying roar of disapproval from Master, who at last was giving Kym attention. Also in the evening Kym liked to share his attentions between us and commuted from lap to lap, quite sure that his bulky purring weight was essential to human happiness.

He would lurk on the hearthrug, innocent. Watching. Then, just as our attention was focussed on anything but him he would leap.

He might land under the paper, purring, to lie in wait, occasionally reaching out his paw to tap the hand that turned the pages. He might land in the middle of it, disastrously. He might go right through it like a circus act. Whichever he did, the result was always very satisfying to him, and once the paper reader had stopped being angry, Kym was usually allowed to play the tunnel game.

The tunnel game was heaven and could go on for hours. Our boredom threshold was much lower than Kym's. He could wait endlessly by a minute hole in the garden expecting mice to materialise, occasionally poking a hopeful paw, sure that his wait would be rewarded, quite unaware that this particular hole was there for the clothes post to fit into.

The paper was set up on the floor in a tube, with a ping-pong ball at one end. Kym lurked under the sideboard, his tail end wagging from side to side, as he poised himself to pounce. A rush and a leap and a glorious rustle and he tapped the ball, which sped across the floor.

It was retrieved and set ready again and back under the sideboard he went, lurking there until we thought he had gone to sleep. Just as we relaxed, deciding to go on reading our books, he erupted like a small demon, flying through the tunnel and up over the furniture, until everyone but he was exhausted.

He had one other source of evening entertainment. Television usually baffled him, except for one programme. He adored Tony Hancock! Tony had a very large mouth – which he opened particularly wide as he talked. Kym spent the whole programme on top of the TV set trying to fish out Tony's tongue, which he must have thought was a mouse in a mousehole. By the time the programme ended we were usually hysterical, but not always because of its content. Sid James didn't produce the same effect!

Chapter 4

Kym's one aim in life was to get to safety, as high as possible. If we weren't there, he climbed a tree. Later, on the boat, when it heeled in the wind, he always clung to the upper side, convinced that safety lay here, and not perched more comfortably on the uneasy rocking bunk, where I was busy enduring the voyage and pretending that every bounce was not the last, as I was sure it was.

Safety in the garden meant trees. The apple tree was easy as even I could climb that, but the day that Beagle chased him through three gardens and down the road (as reported to me by neighbours who tried to head Hound off) he really did get stuck, and that time he was not even in our own garden.

Animals have a habit of creating chaos. It is consoling to think that even Royalty has to suffer from the uninhibitedness of dogs and horses, especially when one has been put into an even sillier position than usual. It is rarely possible to salvage dignity, as it is necessary to struggle with something not only in danger from its own position, but in even greater danger from its own terror.

Often a cat up a tree will go higher as people persist in trying to get it down. The noise and the strange humans add to panic, as the animal is convinced that strangers mean harm, and only a stupid animal is born trusting everybody. Most retain a certain wild sense that is very useful.

On this particular day there was my cat, chased by Beagle, right at the tip of the highest tree in the garden next door. A very high tree indeed, its topmost point above their house roof, and that is two storeys high.

I called.

Kym balanced himself on a swaying twig and screamed. The twig trembled under his weight, which at that time was not very much.

I went round to ask if I could trespass and of course everybody was out. By now the noise from the tree was ear-splitting, as not only was Kym yowling, but the birds were mobbing him. I began to worry, as the magpies are killers and might easily blind him, or so terrify him he fell to his death. There seemed little chance even the luckiest cat could survive falling from that height, trying to escape from the attentions of birds that found him unwelcome on their territory.

Also there were nests in the tree and the parent birds were flying up towards the kitten, obviously adding to his terror.

If I threw anything at the birds, Kym would probably imagine I was trying to hit him and that would make matters worse.

He was not concerned with birds. He was concerned with fear. The ground was miles below him and so was I. I was a giant to him anyway, as he only came up to my ankle, and he had to swarm me like a tree, so that now he must appear to be so far from earth that he might as well be on the moon. Everything must be magnified beyond my imagining.

I called to him again.

He was blind and he was deaf. He was pure panic, clinging for his life, swaying in the wind that was needling the branches, blowing my hair and blowing his fur. He hated wind when he was on the ground. Up there, it must feel like a gale.

He was totally unreachable, as even our highest ladder wouldn't be long enough; and I have no head for heights at the best of times, though it is surprising what one can do when pushed.

He was going to fall!

He did fall, slithering a few feet to cling, screeching, in the fork of one of the topmost branches, as far out of my reach as before, a minute ball of black and cream, so tiny that it seemed impossible for him to have climbed so high.

An hour passed.

I went back at intervals. If I called the fire brigade they probably couldn't reach him, as it would need a very long ladder and the tree was at the bottom of the garden, nowhere near the road.

I went home, opened the windows and cooked his fish, hoping that the smell would bring him down. Usually he only had to sniff his dinner and he was there beside me, telling me how hungry he was, sometimes so impatient that he bit my leg to make me hurry, especially if he were having liver. Sometimes he arrived so fast he skidded on the linoleum and hit the opposite wall.

The smell obviously reached him as he yowled more loudly than ever.

I put some of the fish on his plate, and took a fork. I climbed as far as I could up the tree, hoping my neighbours wouldn't mind. They were still out. It wasn't easy to climb, with a plate in one hand, and the fork in my teeth. I felt like a rather crazy Carmen, lacking her rose.

I was seated astride a branch, rattling hopefully, when my neighbours came home. Luckily they too have always had cats, being now on the third since we moved in next to them, so they understood. They also knew that my methods wouldn't work unless I were alone, so they went indoors. It was almost time for my children to come home from school. I didn't think their excitement would help. I wanted Kym down. And I wanted him down quick.

Eventually hunger triumphed.

He began to come down, backwards, clinging tightly. He came very cautiously, looking down anxiously at intervals, exclaiming in dismay because he still hadn't travelled very far. The birds did not falter in their indictment. High above me, near the top of the tree, they persisted with a constant barrage of sound. Their wings and voices kept us unwanted company all afternoon.

Slowly, carefully, the minutes crept by as he slithered and slipped and slid until at last I could reach him, and he was safe, clinging tightly to me, his body trembling, every muscle whipcord tense.

It was a long time before he stopped complaining.

Beagle was more unwelcome than ever. He might be the sweetest dog in the world on his own patch. He was an unmitigated nuisance on mine. His successor still is.

As Kym grew, so his noise grew.

More than anything, he hated rain. If the ground was wet he walked gingerly, flicking the water daintily from each paw, stepping high like a trotting horse, squalling as he went.

If the rain was lashing down, he insisted that the front door was opened, and peered out, suspiciously, mewling crossly at the weather that dared to spoil his day. As we live in the rain shadow, near Manchester, rain was a frequent annoyance in Kym's life.

He walked back down the hall, having decided it was too wet in front for any self-respecting cat to go out. He stomped into the kitchen and very firmly demanded that the back door be opened. It might not be raining there.

It always was.

He never did fathom weather.

Of course, at times, it stopped raining at one door or the other. He obviously felt it might still be raining outside the *other* door, so he confined his walk to a very few feet, ready to dash back if the rain started and determined not to be caught anywhere in the rest of the garden, which might still be enduring a downpour.

He never in all his life ventured far enough after rain to

discover that in fact it was safe to walk quite a distance.

The path puddled, so he usually sat on the porch and surveyed the scene. Should rain start again he would come in and spend his time pacing endlessly up and down the hall, with an astonishingly heavy tread.

He was not a small delicate cat; he weighed a stone when full grown, and had muscles like a dog and a very solid little body. He once startled a neighbour of mine beyond measure by slipping into her house one hot summer day, to lie in the shade on her bed.

She knew she was alone in the house and had not seen or heard him come in. She was appalled to hear a heavy thump in the bedroom above her while she was eating her lunch. She waited, horrified, as footsteps came slowly and heavily down the stairs. Then she heard a familiar waugh and went out to see Kym stalking down her hall as if he owned her house too. He acknowledged her regally, as she often had coffee with me, and walked outside, to come home as he was sure it was time to eat.

He was very like Winnie the Pooh, always ready for a little something. If it weren't provided he stole it – once from his unwitting hostess of that afternoon, finding she had put her lunch to cool on the windowsill beside an open window. It was fish in aspic and very nice too. It was also early closing day. I had to provide a substitute meal for a somewhat indignant and angry friend.

I never did find out who owned the four pork chops that he stole. He refused to eat for two days. I commented to my next door neighbour, who kept two English setters, that I thought he was sickening for something and he was to go to the vet that evening.

'Since you give him pork chops I'm not surprised he won't eat,' she said somewhat acidly, obviously feeling I had idiotic notions about cat diet.

I discovered he had eaten them two days before, under her hedge. She had tried to take them away and got sworn at for her pains, so she left him to it. Someone must have lost their Sunday dinner. It took Kym some days to recover from that particular orgy. Pork in quantity isn't very good for cats, obviously. Even though I was assured by my neighbour that it was most beautifully cooked.

I decided this was a case of ignorance being bliss and made no enquiries. None of my friends complained, so he must have gone foraging afar.

Having discovered my neighbour's home contained a Rayburn which she used in the summer as well as the winter, as it was her only means of cooking, Kym used to commute between our houses. He preferred to bask on her rug by the fire on days when I decided we should stay cold as it was June, and it seemed a crime to waste fuel in summer – a piece of puritan behaviour I still conform to, but don't really understand. It's crazy to freeze in our British climate even if it is nominally mid-June!

Kym in this respect was much more sensible than I.

By the time he was four months old he obviously hadn't heard that Siamese cats were delicate or vicious, though I wasn't at all sure that he wouldn't be short lived. Not because of bad health. By now he was in boisterous health, noisy, lively, active, and so curious that I spent all his life convinced he would end it suddenly and violently by accident.

His first real brush with death, once he had recovered from his initial illness, occurred when he was about five months old. He was half grown and rather gawky, an adolescent cat, with all his seal points. He had just been neutered, as the last thing one wants living in the house is a full male Siamese. Their yells for a mate are deafening, and their persistence is impossible to live with. Their habits are often revolting indoors.

He came into the kitchen crying. Not his usual robust shout, but a fretful unhappy wail that said very plainly that something was wrong. I picked him up. His paw and his mouth were dark and slimy and he smelled most odd.

I went outside and discovered that Kenneth was creosoting the fence.

'Has Kym been around?' I asked.

'He was here a few minutes ago', he said, and went on with his work. I sniffed the creosote tin and then went in and sniffed the cat. He had dipped his paw in the tin, and then licked it. Tongue, palate, mouth and paw were all smothered in the horrible stuff.

I flew to my very well thumbed reference book, Brian Vesey Fitzgerald's book on cats which contains practically everything that any cat owner could possibly wish to know. I looked under POISONS and there it was. Creosote. I looked at my cat, wondering if he would survive and how much he had taken into him.

I rang the vet.

'There's not much you can do, as there isn't an antidote', he said, not at all reassuringly. 'All you can do is to give him as much milk as he will take; keep on giving it to him. And bath him to get the stuff off.'

It was a weekend. We had my husband's parents staying with us, and the children were around, and totally dismayed.

'Will he die?' they asked.

I didn't know. I thought the answer probably was yes, but I was going to do all I could. I gave him milk, which he drank eagerly. And more milk. It all went down.

And then I tried to bath him.

The only possible place was in the sink, as that was high, with the draining-board beside it on which I could put a towel. Knowing cats, I shut the doors and windows and instructed everyone to keep out.

I filled the sink with warm soapy water, found the nail brush, and grabbed the cat. I put him in the water. He exploded from it, showering me and the kitchen with foamy drops as he shook himself vigorously, and stood, minute and defiant, spitting at me in fury for daring to subject him to such treatment.

I hadn't any choice.

I managed to catch him and once more put him in the sink and scrubbed him, holding him tightly in spite of scratches and bites. He had to be clean or he would just lick more of the stuff, and that could well be fatal, even if it wasn't already.

The noise he made was sufficient to convince me that at that instant he was nowhere near death. He was the angriest small beast I had ever seen, and had become a jungle cat, wild as any wildcat, enraged to such a state that it was very difficult to cope with him.

I rolled him in the towel, holding it tightly against me and filled the sink with warm water to rinse him.

It was at this point a friend called, came into the kitchen and stared, and then began to laugh.

'I've never heard of anyone bathing a cat', she said, between shouts of amusement.

It was the final straw for Kym, who could never bear being laughed at. He sank his teeth into my wrist. Deep.

Some hours later, dry, comfortable, and fluffy from his immersion, looking as angelic as any kitten could look, he forgave me and climbed into my lap for his usual evening sleep. He drank more milk at bedtime, and seemed very little the worse for his adventure. Next morning he was hungry and fed greedily. I rang our vet and told him all was well.

'You were very lucky', he said.

We didn't know it, but that was to become our password over the years. Kym had the same vet for all of his life, and spent more time there than any of my other cats have ever done, always due to his own impetuosity.

Chapter 5

Most animals learn by experience, but to a cat in a human world there are so many different experiences that often one lesson doesn't stand him in good stead, as a slightly different situation may have the same results.

To Kym, tins contained food, and food was meant for him. He could jump anywhere, on to any shelf or table, and could find a way of getting food from any container. Arthur the TV cat didn't invent the use of a paw for food.

Kym knew about it long before Arthur was born.

A paw, dipped into the milk jug, brought him a rewarding drink. I had to learn always to remove milk jugs and cream jugs from the table. A large ham once provided him with material for an assault course. I heard a shout and found my husband busy separating Kym from the big piece of ham I had cooked to cut and come again.

We cut off the ham where the kitten had anchored himself. Before we had even finished, he was back again at the other end.

Meat, if he got at it, was dragged to the floor. Fish was definitely his prerogative, not ours. When we had fish and chips after a weekend away, to save me from extra cooking when I was tired, we always had to set aside a small portion from each of us for Kym or the resulting row was unendurable, and we were kept busy fielding him from our plates.

Shut him outside the door, and the noise was deafening. Put him in the garden, and he promptly came and sat on the windowsill, bellowing. All we could do was to make sure he had his share.

At times, when I was alone in the house, I sat reading

with my plate of food on my lap, not being addicted to the extra work involved in laying a table just for one, and not needing all the etceteras. Kym would be on the floor, watching for his moment. When I was distracted by my book, a lean paw snaked out, a long claw grabbed a piece of meat and he dived under the sideboard away from me.

I never learned!

Once, after I had endured an operation, the family gave me my dinner in bed as I was just out of hospital. My husband, who is rather a splendid cook and puts me to shame, had made roast pork, with all the trimmings. Kym decided to come and help me convalesce. It was no use banning him from the room as the noise he made when shut out was enough to send any invalid back to hospital.

He sat on my bed while I ate. I wasn't reading; I was busy balancing the tray and trying not to drop food on the bedclothes. The long paw kept angling towards my meat. He watched every movement, and finally, annoyed because I wasn't getting much into me as I was too busy fielding my plate, I gave him a hard tap across the paws.

He turned his back, stalked with total dignity to the bottom of the bed, and sat there, tail twitching angrily, while I finished my meal. It was very hard not to laugh, but that would only have added to his annoyance and wasn't really fair. He didn't forgive me until supper time.

He used his paw, often, to test the temperature of his own food. He liked it tepid, but not ice cold from the refrigerator. He was very particular about the heat of the food he ate. He touched it gingerly, feeling it to see if he could actually stand the food in his mouth. If it were too hot, he eased a small piece off the plate, on his claw, like eating winkles with a pin, and kept it there for a few seconds before finally eating it, apparently having found by trial and error that the food gradually cooled.

He loved eating cornflakes in this way, not because they were hot, but apparently because he found it enormously satisfying to spear each flake and lift it to his mouth gently, savouring the taste. Then he drank the milk, having finished all the solids.

He preferred coley to meat, and there was only one brand of proprietary catfood that he would eat. He would rather die than touch all the other carefully prepared and tested foods. They just weren't edible as far as he was concerned. He loved mince and brown bread; and the giblets from the chickens; and a little liver, not too much, as too much was constipating if cooked and had the reverse effect if raw.

If I were reduced to giving him tinned food, he preferred to starve. Nothing would make him eat something if he didn't like it. I could put it down for meal after meal. All he did was to go foraging in the neighbourhood and steal. Once he slipped in next door and stole Dusky's dinner; once he went across the road and stole from their ginger cat. Once he went down the road and stole from another friend of mine.

So I gave up all tinned foods except the one and even that he would only eat on rare occasions. Fresh food or else, every time. Not a delicate feeder, but a very fussy one. And no way for me to win. Ever.

For all that, tins remained a source of fascination to Kym. When we had cream out of a tin or out of a plastic container, he was allowed to lick the remains. This was bliss, so that he crouched, reminding me of Harold Monro's poem, *Milk for the Cat*. Monro wrote;

> A long dim ecstasy holds her life;
> Her world is an infinite shapeless white.

Kym, licking cream, was exactly like that. Eyes half closed, intent on savouring the utmost from the wonderful, far too rare taste, he was obviously translated into a world beyond our understanding. He was all sensation, delighting in each second, prolonging it for endless minutes, until the carton was so clean it might have been scrubbed.

Only then did he return to the present, and lick my hand, and purr deeply and satisfyingly, a noisy continuing rumble that showed how much he had enjoyed his treat. On birthdays, which were on 2 March, he always had a spoonful of cream to himself. Yet milk was usually ignored, unless it was stolen from the jug or mixed with cornflakes.

Tins were to steal from as well, no matter what the contents. Baked beans, sardines, pilchards, corned beef; if he found an empty tin in went his prospecting paw, to be tasted when he had managed to get some of the contents smeared on to it.

Which must have been how he came to have one of the most idiotic adventures of his life, and one of the most aggravating.

It was one of those days.

Nothing had gone right from the time I got up. I had been greeted by fretful calls from the twins' bedroom and found them both covered in spots.

Our elder son was just back at school after some spotty children's infection so it wasn't surprising, but it was annoying, as I had had a busy day planned. I cancelled my plans, waited for the doctor, and went into the kitchen where I found the fire out and water in the hearth.

The boiler had developed a leak.

So it was also cold and I was waiting for the plumber.

And that day every hawker in the district and the Avon lady decided to call, so that I trogged upstairs with drinks and jigsaw puzzles and crayons and books to crayon and books to read, and more drinks, and downstairs to answer the doorbell sure it was the doctor or the plumber and increasingly annoyed because it was neither.

Finally the twins went to sleep and I collapsed into a chair, still doctorless and plumberless, and decided to write to my sister.

I had also managed to burn the lunch, through a loud yell from upstairs of 'Mummy, I've spilt my drink'.

By the time the sheets were changed and the floor mopped up, the lunch was only a memory of what it might have been and we had scrambled eggs on toast instead.

Kym had vanished early that morning, as it was a moderately bright day in spite of the cold. But he ought to have been home long ago and I added a mild worry about him to all the other irritations of the day.

'One thing, nothing else *can* go wrong', I had just written, being unwise, when Kym came down the front path, crying frantically.

He was walking in the oddest way, every leg stiff, and I couldn't imagine what on earth was wrong.

I picked him up.

He was glistening from top to tail, mouth, front legs, chest, hind legs, and tail, all solid and shining, gummed together. He was smothered, thick, in VARNISH that had set like a rock on him.

I rang the vet.

There was a small silence and a deep sigh.

'Only Kym could do a thing like that,' the voice at the other end of the line said. 'All we can do is shave him under anaesthetic. You'd better get him in quick and I'll sedate him and we'll do it in the morning.'

The wails were only outdone by the noise the twins were making, demanding to know what was going on. Inevitably my husband had the car, as he had had a meeting which might go on late. He very rarely took it in. Only on those days did I ever seem to need it. It was on one of those days that our twin son managed to break his nose.

I told his secretary what had happened. She was a genius at getting messages wrong, and being totally unable to understand what had really happened although I did try to make it as plain as possible, she told my husband I wanted the car as I had varnished the cat.

Not very surprisingly he decided I had gone out of my mind and was playing a very untimely practical joke on him, which he most certainly didn't appreciate while he was at work. He ignored the message.

I had needed both him and the car as someone had to be there for the doctor and the plumber.

Not to mention the twins who weren't old enough to leave on their own.

Time passed and everyone came, but no car. I met it at the usual time at the door, showed my very startled husband the cat, asked him to keep an eye on both supper and twins, leaped into the car and set off.

We made excellent time for the whole ten yards from our house to the main road. I had forgotten about rush hours. Kym was as unhappy as any cat could be. He yelled at the top of his voice, non-stop, as he was driven at a pitiful crawl all of the five miles to the vet, right along one of the busiest roads in the area. There is a fifty mile an hour limit, but whoever thought that up was joking. We were never out of second gear.

The vet was speechless when he saw the cat.

I left Kym, wondering which of our neighbours had found a tin of varnish spilled all over the place. It must have travelled too, as Kym had obviously walked about for some time, dripping varnish. He had the stuff all over all four paws.

He had also tried to lick it off and his mouth was gummed solid.

And you can't dip cats in solvent.

I rang next morning and was told I could have my cat back at two. I asked the neighbour who had lost her fish to Kym if she would come with me and hold him. He couldn't stand the cat basket, and the journey to the vet had been tricky, apart from the rush hour.

That particular vet is on a very busy main road, opposite the cemetery. Visits to him were always trying, as there is difficulty in parking, difficulty in crossing the road and inevitably surgeries were during rush hours. We now have a local vet, which is much more convenient. I was sorry to change – but we only have a five-minute trip now in an emergency.

I parked outside the cemetery, managed at last to cross the road, and went in to get my cat. He was still hazy from the anaesthetic, swearing like a particularly vicious trooper, slashing at the girl who tried to give him to me.

She refused to handle him. He was a horrible animal.

I spoke to him softly.

'Kym.'

He was out of the cage in an instant, into my arms, trying to get under my clothing, purring, talking excitedly, pushing his paw down the neck of the dress I was wearing. I put on his collar and lead and held him and soothed him.

He was almost totally bald.

There was a patch of fur between his ears and a tiny saddle round his back. There was no fur on any of his legs. His tail was stripped except for a poodle clump of fluff at the end. There was a little fur underneath him. His whiskers had gone and his mouth looked sore.

But there was no doubt whatever that he was overjoyed to see me. He had endured all kinds of horrible things since I left him behind, and he felt very peculiar indeed, still woozy from the anaesthetic.

I stood waiting to cross the road.

Two cars approached, slowed down and the drivers stared. A lorry, hurtling towards us, changed gear with a screech that upset Kym, and an astounded face looked at me and my cat. The driver rolled his eyes heavenward with a 'There's one born every minute' look on his face, and drove on, obviously sure this idiot woman had had her Siamese clipped like a poodle for fashion's sake.

We got across the road at last and Kym spent the journey telling my friend just how terrible it had all been. He tried to stand, but his legs still didn't belong to him, and when he got home he weaved up and down for hours, trying to get some strength back into himself.

Needless to say, he was starving. Nothing made any difference to his appetite except serious illness.

He looked extremely odd for months. Luckily it was summer, and he did not have to endure the cold.

By the time the fur had grown again he had matured.

This proved to be a pity, as he promptly developed an Emperor complex. He was by then a very large cat for his breed, with a magnificent coat which darkened at every moult, so that the cream was turning to a tawny brown on his hind quarters. The seal points were richly black, and his crossed vivid blue eyes in his all-black mask gave him a saturnine expression, which he accentuated often by flattening his ears.

He had been mercilessly chased by other cats when he was small, and he determined to get his own back now. The only cat he tolerated was coal black Tigger, a farm cat that had been imported by the family who lived two doors away from us and who was the same age as Kym.

Kym and Tigger became the best of friends, playing together, sleeping together under bushes, hunting together. Kym would shout from our garden and a few minutes later Tigger came running in, though he would never allow me to touch him.

Their friendship continued all summer.

They were charming together, playing hide and seek through the shrubs in the garden, racing one another up the trees, indulging in endless games of touch and run, chasing one another's tails, or lying close against one another under the catmint, which they both loved to such an extent that it died off, unable to stand their attentions.

Then, one night, Kym failed to come home. This was totally unusual. He was always there, starving, yelling at me for being so slow, nipping me impatiently if he didn't have his food put down *this instant*. He had a voracious appetite which happily encompassed theft, his own food,

Tigger's food and mice.

There was no sign of him.

At that time everyone knew everyone in the road, so that when I asked my neighbours if they had seen Kym there was a general alert, by word of mouth, over the garden fences, and everyone hunted their gardens.

No sign of him anywhere.

Then Tigger's owners turned up to ask if Kym and Tigger were in our house, as Tigger had vanished too.

We hunted together. We went into the fields, calling, but the fields then were a large area, with crops growing, with cattle, and with all kinds of wild life, including a fox or two. Had they fallen victim to the fox? We didn't know. I suspected Kym would have fought valiantly and might have been hurt but not killed by a fox. He was a great battler, now chasing every cat but Tigger off his territory.

There was no sign of the cats.

We parted despondently, wondering if they had been stolen. My mother had recently lost a beautiful tawny cat in a Croydon suburb and the police had been sure that he had been picked up by thieves as he was one of a large number that vanished in that area. Illegal vivisection laboratories pay well for cats. And their fur makes gloves.

The thought was not conducive to sleep and by five in the morning, as soon as it was light, I was out again, calling through the fields, and searching the gutters where a dead cat might be put, having been hit by a car.

I met Tigger's owner, out on the same quest. We looked together, but no cats appeared.

I got breakfast and saw everyone off, feeling defeated. I hate an animal to die, but I hate even more not knowing what has happened to it. I was just getting ready to go shopping when a small whirlwind stormed in, yelling at me, coming so fast he banged into me, and so hungry he bit me several times on my way to the refrigerator to get his food, which he bolted as if he had never been fed in his life.

65

He then sat on the windowsill and declaimed.

A few minutes later the doorbell rang. It was my neighbour asking if Kym had come home yet. She knew where the cats had been. Her son had opened up the garage that morning to get his bicycle to go to school. They had no car, and he left later than our children.

There was a small explosion from a packing case at the back of the garage. The two cats had gone in there and gone to sleep. No one had heard them, a fact I found hard to believe until the same thing happened again years later, and I found Kym in a neighbour's garden shed. She hadn't heard him, but I, who was listening, had. Neighbours of hers on the other side had thought he was in the garden, calling, and had ignored the noise.

After that whenever the cats went missing we searched the sheds, the garages and the greenhouses thoroughly as sometimes they would be curled up warmly, and be deaf to all calls.

Kym's friendship with Tigger lasted until early the next year when my neighbours, who were going on holiday, suggested that I should look after Tigger while they were away and they would do the same for Kym later.

Tigger could sleep in his own house and I was to have the key. I thought I could feed the two cats together in my kitchen. This seemed even more probable when as soon as the taxi had taken the family away, Tigger landed on my doorstep suggesting I might feed him. By the end of the three weeks he came for me when he was hungry, or wanted to go indoors, or it was wet, and led me to his home, waiting for me to put him inside.

He never was fed in my kitchen for the simple reason that as soon as I put food down for him, Kym attacked him, as far as I could see out of jealousy. Tigger was lonely, and had jumped to my lap.

That was unforgivable. No one else was entitled to my lap. Kym sprang, spitting, and Tigger fled. Thereafter he received the same treatment as all the other cats that dared encroach on Kym's territory.

Tigger remained very lonely, but I could never fuss him anywhere near our house. I had to take him into his own home and cuddle him there. He would only eat sitting on my lap. If I put the food down and left it, it was untouched when I returned, but so long as I held him and comforted him, he would relax and feed.

Feeding Tigger often took half an hour, as he demanded affection. He was used to it from his owners and missed it horribly. They found when they came to do the same for Kym, that he insisted on attention too. Cats are only aloof if no one bothers about them.

I fed Tigger often after that, but I always had to take care that Kym was nowhere near when I fussed the other cat. And Tigger, who had never come to me, continued to come to me only when his family were away. In between whiles I could go jump the moon. But as soon as the taxi had gone, he was on my doorstep, demanding my attention, knowing that I would feed him and see that he didn't get wet.

Kym's fights remained a major problem all his life. Most cats tried to defend themselves, so that he was constantly bitten. Many of the bites abscessed. Injections became part of our lives, and those trips to the vet.

On one occasion I tried to stop a fight. I was about to go to London for a long publicity tour for *The Running Foxes* and I knew that if Kym were bitten and it abscessed, the family would not spot the injury until the abscess had really taken hold. I was by now so used to them that I knew the early symptoms, and could get one injection instead of three to clear it up, as it hadn't developed by then.

Kym was fighting the enormous tabby tom from the farm. The yells and screams alerted me. I raced across the road and grabbed Kym just as he was chasing the other cat. He must have thought Tabby had returned and jumped him. He lashed round, sank his teeth into my hand, and raked his claws down my arm.

It was entirely my own fault as I hadn't spoken. I had just grabbed. No animal will stand for that.

As soon as I spoke he realised what he had done and leaped into my arms, pushing his face against mine, patting me anxiously with his paw, as if to say he hadn't known and he hadn't meant to. He rolled against me, purring.

He had been bitten, quite badly.

We both had injections that time. I was amused to read a few days later that the Prime Minister's wife, Mary Wilson, had suffered the same treatment from her Siamese cat – and probably for the same reason. Our son got caught the same way a year or two after.

Some years later the same tabby came into our road. By then he was a very slow old cat, in rather bad condition. He ambled into the sunshine, and Kym began to stalk him, tail swishing, shouting his challenge.

Tabby gave Kym one look, and dropped, full length, in the middle of the road, lying absolutely still, stretched out, nothing moving but his eyes.

Kym stared at him and circled him, not knowing what to make of a cat that didn't try to fight back.

Tabby didn't move.

Kym circled him again, this time silently. Nothing happened at all.

Puzzled, Kym sat down and washed his shoulder, hard, still watching the older cat, and then, as again nothing happened, he put up a hind leg to wash that.

Tabby's indolence was forgotten.

He streaked away, faster than I had believed possible, while Kym was still trying to make out what to do. Tabby vanished into next door's garden and, as I had been standing near our gate watching them, I called Kym in and fed him, feeling the old boy deserved to get away without trouble, as he had obviously shown that he had no intention of fighting, and most probably wasn't capable of it.

I never did find out which cat was the cause of Kym's worst injury as I had a horrible suspicion that the other cat might be dead, and I did not dare ask questions. Kym came limping home one bright sunny day with his ear bitten through, his paw very badly bitten, and an enormous chewed hole on his head, right between the ears.

He had several injections but the head wound abscessed and nothing we could do would get it clear.

Finally the vet operated, removing all the flesh down to the bone, and I had to bathe that every few hours to try and keep it from healing over until all the poison had gone. He couldn't go out either as we could not risk further injury. That might have been fatal.

After that I developed an early warning system and as soon as I heard Kym's battle cry, I raced out to fetch him in, and tried to ensure that we had no further fights of that magnitude. He might have tangled with our stray, an immense black and white tom that all cat owners worried about, as he was in a dreadful state, with discharging eyes and nose and cankered ears, but he was so fast that none of us could get him; not even the R.S.P.C.A. inspector managed to catch him.

We finally caught him when he was very old and obviously dying. I asked the vet to come and give him his final shot, after bringing him into our garage and warming him and feeding him for what must have been the first time for years. He was seething with fleas and lice, and had an appalling injury that must have come from a car, on one side. He had been crying round the houses like a dispossessed demon for weeks before I managed to entice him in with catfood. He was too weak to run.

Kym himself had gone by then. He and the old cat must have been about the same age.

I felt sorry for the stray, wandering for all those years, with no home and no food given to him, and no one to care about him. He was neither truly wild nor tame, but one of the outcasts caused by man, as his owners had moved away and left him behind to roam like a wild beast for the rest of his life. He was around, uncaught, for more than eight years, and as wary as any wild beast in the woods.

The Mrs Mopp I had then, who was a darling who cleaned up for us for more than ten years, once commented that her idea of hell was to be like the old cat, unwanted, and her idea of heaven was to be a cat like Kym, in a house where he was treasured.

'I think I'll be a Siamese next time round,' she said one day, watching him bask by the fire while we both put our coats on to brave the snow.

Chapter 6

In Kym's early days he rarely came away with us, although we had the caravan then. It was a touring van; about sixteen feet long, and not all that roomy by the time everyone was in it. Either our neighbour looked after Kym, or another neighbour, a friend down the road who thought the world of him.

She apparently started by coming to the house to feed him, bringing his meal in a big straw carrier bag embroidered with raffia flowers that was so much part of her that I still associate it with her whenever I hear her name, though she moved long ago.

Kym hated being alone.

He jumped into the basket, and waited for her to pick it up and take him with her. Finally, after two days of this, she did, and after that whenever she looked after him, she collected him in the morning and took him back at night. When they reached her house he sat in the basket, waiting to be released, and prowled contentedly, commenting endlessly on everything she had.

She missed him so much when she moved that she now has her own cat, named Kym after her first attachment to ours. We missed her too and we decided Kym would have to go into kennels when we were away.

When he was about three years old, the family divided for their holidays. By now my husband had a small two-berth Silhouette yacht, and he and the boys went cruising in it. It wasn't big enough for all of us, and I don't like boats at all, so my daughter, my sister and I went pony trekking, based at Windermere, where we had glorious weather and glorious rides.

Our neighbours with Tigger were away and my other friend had now moved, so Kym went to kennels.

I did not know what establishments there were in the area, and got the address from friends. I went to look before I booked him in and was shown a magnificent chalet with a run, where I was assured he would live for the week, and would be fed like a king.

I left without any worries.

When we returned and the children were all back at school, I went to collect him. There was another cat in the chalet.

'Oh, we moved him this morning,' the kennel owner said, and went through a little wicket gate.

I followed.

'This is private,' she said frostily.

'He happens to be my cat,' I said with equal frostiness. 'And I want to get him myself.'

'We don't allow clients round here,' she said icily.

That could only mean one thing and that was that the place wasn't fit to be seen, as no one at all objects to decent premises being inspected.

She couldn't push me away, so she had to lead the way.

I followed her into a small garden shed, round the sides of which were stacked dozens of rabbit hutches. Inside, on sawdust, were the cats. The sawdust stank. The shed stank. Kym was lying dejectedly in the only clean corner of his hutch, with congealed food on the plate in front of him. That plate hadn't been washed for days either.

I lifted him out. He smelled abominable. I paid, telling the owner that this was the last time my cat would be left there, and that I would never recommend the place to anyone. It was appalling.

The chalet was obviously window dressing, a reception cage which was inhabited for exactly as long as it took the owner's engine noise to die away.

I rolled Kym in newspaper. He wasn't fit to touch. He tried to wash, all the way home, worrying me intensely as he seemed to have no energy. The only noise he had made in greeting was fretful, but I thought perhaps he had cried so much for us that he had lost his voice, which can happen.

I washed him thoroughly and dried him and laid him by the fire.

He didn't eat, and then I realised that some of the mess on him was from his own saliva. He was ill.

We went straight to the vet.

'Has he been in kennels?' he asked.

I told him where.

'We've had eleven from there,' he said, as he filled the syringe. 'And one of them's dead.'

It wasn't at all reassuring. Kym had obviously been ill for at least two days. His eyes were mattering, and so was his nose, and he refused all food. I wished we had never gone away.

It was our kitten fight all over again. Glucose and water every half hour. Bathing eyes and mouth and nose. Trying to interest him in staying alive; feeding him chicken jelly and beef broth and marrow bone broth which I made.

He didn't move from the chair in which I had put him for ten days. He seemed to have nothing inside him to come out. Everyone came home and looked at him and went silently about the house.

He didn't even lift his head to feed.

He came, lying in the car in a box on blankets and hot water bottle, to the vet daily for injections. We were now one of a queue, not allowed in the waiting room because of infection. We stood outside, holding cats, wrapped in towels, inside our coats, to keep them warm. There were ten of us when we started. There were more by the time we had finished, but not many more, because several of the cats failed to survive.

They had all been kennelled in the same place.

Cat 'flu is the very devil as it is so infectious. In a way it is not really fair to blame kennels as a carrier can infect every cat there. But kennels can keep the cats clean and can call in vets. Most owners would prefer to pay a vet bill than to collect a very sick cat. And I prefer decent premises and would happily pay for them. We have splendid kennels near us now.

By the ninth day I asked the vet to call, as the cat was so ill I didn't want to move him. He came and looked, and said,

'He's suffered too much. If there's no improvement by tomorrow . . .'

He didn't need to finish. I was already wondering if it were kind to keep him alive.

We all walked around as if *we* were under sentence of death. No one felt like eating at all. The children went to bed and we sat and read. I held Kym on my lap. He stared dully at nothing and didn't want to talk, or to wash or to move.

He lay, scarcely breathing.

My husband looked at the cat.

'We can't do him any further harm', he said. 'What about trying a little brandy?'

We gave him half a teaspoonful from a spoon. It would have been better to give him diluted spirit from a dropper, but we didn't know that then.

He didn't even try and resist.

All the brandy went down and I put him gently on the chair again, knowing that tomorrow was the end.

A few minutes later, I heard a movement. Kym had sat up, and very groggily, was trying to wash himself. I went over and sat on the edge of the chair beside him, and he tried to scramble into my lap. I lifted him into his haven, and dripped a little glucose into him. He swallowed without my having to stroke his throat, and then managed a very out of practice rusty purr.

In the morning he lapped up a little marrow bone broth, and when the vet arrived, long-faced, expecting to have to put the cat down, he was greeted by a yowl and a purr, not very loud, but plainly a cat-on-the-mend noise, so that we celebrated with a cup of coffee and our vet went away delighted that this patient at least had not eluded him.

Kym recovered in time for us to celebrate Christmas that year by taking him away to my parents' new home in Bexhill. He went out into the garden on Christmas Day and failed to come back.

He rarely left the garden, and we could not imagine what had happened. Needless to say there was no chance of anyone settling to Christmas tea with the cat missing. We went to look for him, sure his voice would call us.

I went one way, the boys another, my daughter down towards the sea, my husband up to the top of the estate and my father went down the road that led to the shops.

We searched for nearly an hour and I had just given up when I heard Kym yowling and found my father holding him somewhat awkwardly. My father was very angry indeed.

Not, it transpired, with the cat.

He had heard Kym answer his call from behind a hedge in a garden. My father had gone in and picked up the cat, and come out again, to be met by an irate lady who was passing by, who accused him of cat stealing and threatened to call the police!

Kym meanwhile didn't know my father all that well and added to the illusion by struggling and complaining. The lady had accompanied them up the hill, my father trying to explain what had happened.

I met them, saw Kym, and he leaped out of my father's arms into mine and at once began his greeting ceremony, this time about twice as ardently as usual. There was no doubt as to whose cat this was. The accuser went away, but my father erupted off and on all the evening, asking plaintively if we thought he *looked* like a cat thief. Not being sure what thieves do look like, we found this a bit hard to answer. It turned out that Kym had been chased by a dog.

Our next Christmas with Kym was even more fraught, as that year our daughter volunteered to look after two of the school mice. Cyril and Ethel were brown mice, living in a metal cage and she should have known from the start that it would be a trying three weeks.

Kym smelt mice.

MICE!

We put the cage in her bedroom; mice don't smell if the cage is scrupulously clean, and it was the only door that Kym couldn't open if he tried. He sat outside the door and howled and Cyril and Ethel had frequent attacks of nerves, rushing dementedly round the cage, diving for cover under the metal foil that lined the bottom.

On New Year's Eve, when we had gone to bed extremely late (or very early on New Year's Day), Cyril escaped from the cage. He was always very bothered by the cat so he took steps to protect himself.

The cage was on a card table pushed into the angle of the wall. On it were sausage sticks which we used to clean out the corners, and mousefood in a polythene bag, kept handy.

Kym, when he wasn't shut in one room or another, still spent his time yelling at the door to get in.

I went to wake our daughter, and glanced at the table. It was minutes before I could speak. She woke up to find me helpless with laughter, gazing at poor Cyril who had built himself a fortress, three sausage sticks thick and twelve high, beautifully aligned, with the two corners of the wall defending him from the rear.

Beside him, higher than he was, was a mouse mountain of mousefood, which he had obviously carried in all night before making himself secure. It would only need one swipe of Kym's paw to overthrow his defences, and he looked so funny, glaring defiance at me from behind his fortification, that it was all we could do to get him out and put him back with Ethel.

They embraced and went to earth under the tin foil.

All went well until the last day. I had promised to take the mice in their cage back to school in the lunch hour; we were to rendezvous outside the biology lab, where the mice lived. I put the cage on the dining room table, as I thought Kym was safely in the garden. He was, but the window was open.

I went to get the car out of the garage.

I came back to find Kym trying his best to rip the cage apart, the only sign of Cyril and Ethel being two tiny mounds under the foil.

Luckily it was a very strong cage.

I took them back. Cyril and Ethel refused to come out from down under for nearly three weeks. As soon as the cage was clean they scurried back into cover again, obviously sure that the giant noisy demon would come and carry them off.

After that the family did agree.

No more mice, however much the biology mistress blandished. School pets are a very good idea but they do cause problems in the holidays. Especially as only animal lovers will take them on, and most animal lovers already have pets of their own.

Kym was rather sorry that the mice had gone. Obviously the smell of them lingered, as he decided to live on the card table where the cage had stood for some days, and think of the smell and remember, even if he never had had the chance he needed. While he sat there he regaled us with his thoughts.

I often wished I could understand them.

Chapter 7

There were many ways in which I could understand Kym, as one grows to know an animal well, and to interpret his actions. One of my major occupations during his lifetime was to listen for that wicked yell that signified his intention of fighting.

His fights were too dangerous, and far too expensive, as there was no quarter shown by either animal. He had many enemies; or perhaps he made them. I was never sure.

He was neutered, but that made no difference, as he was never fighting for a mate. All his battles were territorial.

He fought Sandy, the ginger cat opposite us, whenever they met. So much so that Sandy's master, if he saw Kym, threw handfuls of earth at him to discourage him from coming into the garden. Never mind that it was Sandy's garden. Kym didn't care a whisker about that.

They battled throughout Sandy's life.

And then one day Sandy, who was ill and old, went to the vet and didn't come back. His family were very fond of him, and were upset, as one always is when losing an animal that has been part of the household for years.

That afternoon Sandy's master arrived in the kitchen, carrying Kym, who had always run from him before. Kym had haunted the garden all morning; had gone to Sandy's owner and rubbed round his legs, purring, and had been most reluctant to leave him. He had never before allowed himself to be picked up.

I made coffee and we marvelled at the mind of a cat, wondering why Kym had behaved in this way, which seemed totally uncanny. Whether he knew that Sandy was dead and no longer owned the garden, and was staking a new claim, or whether he was just being sympathetic.

I didn't believe that cats could sense death. It seemed highly improbable. Years later, I was to change my mind.

Kym's battles were liable to lead me into awkward situations, as I always tried to prevent them from becoming too lethal. Another of his hates was a giant tabby from somewhere down the road. A friend of mine used to watch them encounter one another, stalking one another before actually engaging in open warfare.

On one particular winter morning our younger son, who had lost his heart to a herd of Jersey cows and went up to help look after them, had gone out at six in the morning, just before Christmas, and had accidentally let Kym out. He wasn't allowed out in the dark. Too many tom cats were around.

I was half asleep when I heard that unmistakable battle yell. It could only be Kym. I grabbed my dressing-gown, which was long and thick and bright scarlet, and charged out of the house into the darkness, knowing I would be hidden from sight and no one would be up.

Kym was challenging a strange cat on the corner of the road.

I went towards him and strange cat ran.

Kym ran.

I ran.

I felt like a woman in a nursery rhyme. Also I did not feel exactly at ease belting down the road in my nightclothes with a dressing-gown over them and I hoped, very hard, that none of my neighbours went early to work.

I caught up with Kym about four hundred yards down the main road. He was delighted to see me and melted into my arms, purring. Wasn't this fun? Both of us out in the dark.

I didn't think it fun at all. I wasn't very pleased with our son for letting the cat out; or with my highly embarrassing demon cat for starting to fight. I walked back, aware that it was very cold, and that if anyone drew the curtains and looked out, there was I in the light of the street lamps in a bright red dressing-gown, as usual carrying a cat.

We were halfway home when a procession of cars came by, headlamps streaming to light me in their glare. Each car slowed, and I knew that eyes must be staring in sheer amazement.

I reached home to find the postman at our gate.

I attempted, with all the dignity I could muster, to smile and say Good Morning as he handed me the letters. He was obviously convinced I was out of my mind. He knew I was an author anyway, and they are very odd. He always gave me the most peculiar looks when we met after that.

I decided life could never be so embarrassing again, but I was wrong, though on this occasion Kym was an accessory to my discomfiture and not the cause.

He and I were alone in the house, the family being away on its own affairs; my husband was away on business. And when we were all alone Kym slept in my room, as his breathing was reassuring in the night. I never like a totally empty house.

He spent the night curled up in the hollow of my back, under the eiderdown, but outside the blankets. His loud purr reverberated whenever I woke and touched him.

This was heaven.

In the morning he always came to snuggle against my shoulder and look into my eyes and utter deep thoughts, non-stop, till I woke up properly and fed him.

I woke, to the sound of crashing glass.

I looked at my clock.

Three in the morning.

Kym had emerged and was sitting up on the bed, his ears pricked, his eyes watching, his head cocked.

Noises downstairs.

But there was no one else in the house.

The crash sounded again.

Kym looked at me and I looked at him.

He came up the bed into my arms and I sat like a ninny as more noises sounded from downstairs.

I had a telephone extension by my bed. I dialled 999.

I was put through to the police. A reassuring voice asked me for my name and address and assured me a car would be there in five minutes. Meanwhile, lock my bedroom door and on no account go downstairs.

I locked my bedroom door and put on my red dressing-gown and sat with my cat in my arms for the longest five minutes I have ever spent. He wanted protecting. One more crash sounded. There must be a lunatic down there.

The doorbell rang.

I realised then that I had to go downstairs and made the further discovery a few moments later that the bedroom door, which had never before been locked in its life, had jammed, well and truly, and I was locked in. I could throw the police a key but the front door was bolted.

I struggled with the door while Kym yelled that people were ringing the doorbell and didn't I know.

By now any burglars must have taken off at top speed.

A policeman came round to the back of the house and shouted up at the window.

'Are you all right?'

'Yes, but the lock's jammed.'

We both thought it was funny.

Finally I got the door unstuck and wearing Kym, not because I wanted to, but because Noises Downstairs and Men at the Window had totally unnerved him, so that his claws were now jammed into my shoulder, I went down and opened up.

The policemen looked at me, in my red dressing-gown wearing a by now totally incoherent Siamese cat on my shoulder. Kym told them all about it, non-stop, getting louder and louder.

He grew more and more vehement as we toured the house.

No one.

Nothing.

They were very kind and promised to come back if I heard any more noises. Feeling a fool, I went to bed, and read until morning. Kym helped me read, also unable to sleep.

I got up early, and went downstairs, thankful it was day. I drew the curtains, and began to vacuum the floor. The vacuum hose encountered an obstacle which rolled out at my feet.

We had a glass-fronted bookcase which housed the encyclopaedia. I had been looking at a volume the night before, and had left the glass door up, pushed into a slot so that it was at right angles to the bookcase itself.

The greengrocer had delivered late that night and I had built a pyramid of oranges.

They had been unstable and six of them had rolled. Crash on the glass and then to the floor. Six crashes. They were big oranges and had made an alarming noise in the silent house.

Feeling even more of a fool I decided I had better ring the police so that they could close their incident file on me and my goings-on in the night.

'Not to worry', said that reassuring voice. 'We were called out for a poltergeist the other night.'

'What was it?' I asked.

'A mouse, trapped inside the gas fire. You never heard such a noise', he said. 'Your cat would have loved it.'

I could imagine. I knew all about mice. Kym occasionally brought one in alive and released it and whoever coined the phrase as quiet as a mouse had never met one, or heard it in the night, apparently dancing a can-can and cracking Brazil nuts.

I often met 'my' policemen after that. They usually

enquired kindly if I had bought any more oranges, and how was the cat?

I wondered just what they said about us when they got back.

Chapter 8

By the time Kym was three years old we had bought a sixteen-foot touring caravan and had changed our way of life.

Neither of us is addicted to suburban life, as we do not share suburban interests. I prefer country life; riding, walking, out with the dogs. My husband, at that time, longed to return to his major love, boating, but it did not seem feasible, either financially or practically, with a young family.

We could, however, pack up on Friday night, and return on Sunday evening. Saturday morning was devoted to homework; all of us sat writing, my husband dealing with necessary work of his own, I with a new book, the children with their school prep.

After that, all of us were free. Weekends in the caravan meant that we could explore the Lake District; in the school holidays we could go further afield, into Pembrokeshire, up to Scotland, choosing always tiny farms, on marginal land, where the five shillings a night that we paid helped with their minute budgets.

Also, in remote places, we were for the most part extremely welcome, as they rarely saw anyone from one week's end to the other. And being family farms with small children, they were completely tied, not only by the animals.

Kym learned to travel. Travel, for the first few months, was, he was sure, going to end in a visit to the vet. We thought life would be easier if he rode in a cat basket. This was the ultimate horror, shut away, in the dark, unable to see, and no warm hands on him. He yelled, a dervish yell that deafened us all. We felt we had to persist. So he decided to show us, and began to chew the basket. His jaws caught in the wicker. I removed him, mouth sore, ears flat, eyes wild. He never went back in the basket again. It turned into one of those household items, like my marmalade pan, that achieved a life of its own, being borrowed by all my neighbours. It became, in time, a useful fisherman's basket, holding reels and bait and hooks and sinkers, and all the gadgetry one acquires with the hobby. But it never held Kym again.

He travelled, like a dog, with a collar and lead. He managed to slide out of the collar, and once almost leaped out of the car, so that I spent some weeks looking for a puppy harness. He was a large cat, and a puppy harness proved too small, so he was fitted with one that had been made for a small spaniel. This satisfied us both.

He would sometimes deign to walk on his lead. Never the way I wanted to go, but where he wanted to go. He might run up a tree and look at me, eyes wicked, knowing I had to follow and get him down. He wasn't coming down. If I wanted him I could get him.

He might jump on to a wall. If by any chance the road was bordered by a bank, he marched along the top of it, like a child, exclaiming all the way. It seemed to be my fate to be accompanied for ever by an animal that made me look extremely eccentric, but there wasn't any choice. Kym did exactly as he wished and if I looked funny, well, too bad.

He now had to learn a great deal about life away from home, as it had so many hazards. The caravan, he soon discovered, was our base, and his. Inside it, he was safe. Outside it, he was never quite sure what he would see. There were cattle.

He couldn't believe cattle.

He didn't want to believe them. He was exploring, very innocently, as one of our major delights was to stop in a field with a wood beside it and a river near by. Here there were trees to climb, water to paddle in or swim in, and acres of space for cricket, for football, for rushing around and letting off steam without anyone else to bother about.

There were mice; and there were shrews; there was fox smell and stoat smell, and there were birds. Kym could find all he needed to occupy him for hours within a few feet of the caravan.

The wind blew the grass stems. Long dangling ears that bent and tickled his back, so that he stalked them, endlessly, crouching and springing, inventing a ballet of his own as he pounced and patted, sometimes exclaiming in loud comment when he failed to catch a stem; nibbling at it and leaving it when he caught it, only to find another stem enticing him, so that he crept, entranced, concentrating on the movements about him.

A strand of straw was a proxy mouse tail to be killed ruthlessly; to be tapped at as it twisted in the wind. Sometimes there were pieces of string, lying on the grass, abandoned mysteriously, waiting to be teased.

There were holes.

He could spend hours by a hole, hoping that it would yield treasure. He had endless patience if there were even a hint of a beastie down it. He was motionless, wide-eyed, staring, deaf to everything, and the only way to bring him in was to lift him. Invariably he pawed towards the hole trying to hook something out of it, before he was removed from this wonderful exercise.

He always used his paws expressively. If he were sitting on my lap, or lying on my bed and someone moved him away, his paws reached out towards me, scrabbling at the air, demanding that I took him back again and put him beside me, where it was warm and comfortable and safe and he wasn't lonely.

He was sitting by a hole the day he first saw cattle. The wind was unkind to him, and gave no warning, blowing from him to the herd, which was grazing on the far side of a post and wire fence. Kym had found a wonderful hole, a huge hole, right against the fence. He was blissfully unaware of the new fence post waiting to slot into the hole. It was a hole to end all holes, almost big enough for him to get inside, and right at the bottom was a tiny tunnel, in which, he was obviously sure, lurked treasure.

He crouched.

Occasionally he talked, and if the wind blew extra hard, he grumbled.

Something crawled across the hole; perhaps a worm, or a centipede, or a beetle. Whatever it was, Kym had never seen anything like it before. He produced one of his tremendous noises of amazement. The cattle, which move around their grazing area during the day, were just about to graze alongside our fence.

They heard the noise, and being curious, longing to see what had caused such a din, they came, blowing and snorting, heads lifting and tossing, towards the cat.

Kym was petrified.

He stared up at them; at their vast heads, bigger than all his body; at their great brown eyes; at the tree trunk legs and the immense swinging udders. He watched, frozen, unable to move, and then, very cautiously, he turned away, belly on the ground, legs bent, ears flat, tail stretched out behind him, as invisibly as possible; as soundlessly as possible, not a murmur to give him away, hoping the grass was hiding him, showing no telltale to the vast terrifying monsters that might spring and trample and eat him.

I knew he was safe and rather meanly, watched without interfering.

The cows watched too, absolutely mesmerised by his peculiar goings-on. They had never seen anything like it, or any beast that moved in quite such an extraordinary way; for all his caution and his careful creeping, he was as conspicuous as a pheasant in the middle of a country lane. His coat, which darkened with every moult, was now a rich coffee colour; his mask and legs and tail were seal black, and his underparts were cream. He was immensely handsome, and he kept himself immaculate.

He reached the caravan step, and sprang, flying towards me, shouting at the top of his voice, telling me all about the monsters out here that had nearly been the death of him; that had terrified him beyond measure; they were huge. Heaven knows if he had any vocabulary but it always sounded like it and much as I hate humanising animals, this one talked. In any case, one doesn't humanise the animal. We are all animal, with the same needs and desires, for food, for affection, for offspring, for comfort; with the same terrors of the unknown and lurking fear of the dark where devils might still hide. We kid ourselves when we think we are superior. The jungle isn't very far away, even now.

Kym never went out after that when there were cattle about unless I came too. He sat on the windowsill, watching them endlessly, finding them extremely odd. If they came too close to the fence, he swore, vigorously, safely guarded by glass. His noise intrigued them, so that often I would look up from my book and see Kym, enraged, shouting at the top of his voice while on the other side of the fence, a few feet away, an impassive cow stared back at him, apparently unable to tear her eyes away from this small vigorous devil animal that hissed in horror at her, and then beside himself with fury, chattered his teeth.

Later, when he was an older and wiser cat, he learned that the fence kept him safe from the cattle, and he even dared to go a few yards into the cowfield, so long as the herd was grazing safely at the far side of the meadow. Like me, he learned that the cattle seemed to follow the sun, and their movements were unvarying unless they were rounded up by the farmer when he came to inspect them.

Kym also learned that the cows were immensely curious and if he ventured too far, would pack and walk towards him in a menacing group, wanting to see just what he was. He never argued. He always ran.

Many people found it odd that we should travel with a cat.

A dog, yes. Lots of them travelled with one or more dogs, and of course the dogs were delighted to find a cat on any site that we visited. Kym loathed dogs with a deep hatred that lasted all his life. If he came to the vet, we sat, all eyes on us, as he kept up a continuous vicious swear, without apparently stopping for breath. Even if ill, he could fluff his fur, and make his presence heard. I sat in a corner of the waiting room with him tucked firmly into my coat, and, if I could manage it, with his head under my arm so that he couldn't see the dogs.

That did work, as to Kym, anything he couldn't see wasn't there.

The only dog he ever accepted was Radar, the Alsatian who starred some years ago in 'Softly, Softly'. I was writing about him for Annabel and he and his owner came to call. Dorothy said quickly, 'Keep right away from the cat. He's frightened.' Radar never went near but kept the width of the room between them and within an hour Kym relaxed. They spent all day in the same room.

So we watched for site dogs, knowing that if he were chased he would vanish and we might lose him altogether. It was so easy, in the wild, and one never knew if farmers had snares about, or poachers set wire nooses. I have known too many dogs caught by snares meant for rabbits, and have known one farmer so rabid about pets trespassing on his land that he set gin traps. A friend of mine ran her kennels on the far side of this field, and spent most nights trespassing to spring the traps, in case a stray dog came after her bitches and got caught. I knew it wasn't wise to trust to luck where the cat was concerned, and caravanning meant extra vigilance, all the time, for both cat and me.

On one particular site in Scotland, Kym spent all his

94

holiday tied on a long leash to the tow bar, as it was particularly wild, and there were dogs. He could leap inside the van and on to the shelf where he slept if any came too near, and we didn't need to watch him all the time, or lock him in.

I went into the cloakroom there, with showers and cubicles, and room for several people, and overheard two Scotswomen talking, in their soft delightful accents.

'Have ye seen that Siamese cat?'

'Och, that belongs to the Englishman' was the answer, said with such total scorn that I felt more abroad than I ever had on the continent or in America. I was delighted when, next day, a Scottish family came in with an even larger Siamese cat, that went everywhere with them. Tai and Kym became friends and it was very funny to see them, one either side of an imaginary mousehole, tails quivering, erect, their rear ends as expressive as their faces.

They also conversed, which was even funnier, with Kym's voice noisier and more vociferous and Tai occasionally commenting in a much gruffer tone.

On another occasion we arrived at a farm and asked to stay the night, and had just settled ourselves when the farmer's wife came to see that we had all we needed. She took one look at the cat and vanished without another word. I went across later to speak to her husband and asked if they minded the cat being on the farm, as if so, we'd move on.

'It wasn't that,' he said. 'We had a cat the living image of yours. He was run over on the road and killed only a week ago. Seeing yours upset her all over again.'

I promised to try and keep the cat out of sight, but she came back next day to pet and fondle him, and to ask if we knew where she could find a replacement for hers. We were very careful to see that Kym didn't go near the road which, though only a country lane, carried extremely fast traffic that zipped past us in the night, going heaven knew where.

Kym, like us, had his favourite places, and one of these was also one of ours. At that time we often went for the weekend to Plas Coch, in Anglesey. It is now a very big commercial site, but then it was very small. Only a few vans were dotted around the grounds of an old Elizabethan manor house.

It enchanted us as the gardens, though overrun and almost wild, held memories of former times when the house had been a stately home. There was a walled garden, now high with uncut grass, with the remains of fig trees and peach trees, of lavender and thyme. It had once been a quiet retreat. No one ever came there now. I often took Kym on his lead and read a book while the family went on more adventurous outings. I usually forgot to read and lay in the grass, just watching.

There was plenty to watch: birds and mice; a sparrow-hawk hunting; an owl roosting in daylight, mobbed by little birds. Now the walls have gone and the place is a children's playground, and the rhododendrons have been torn down to widen the road so that ever larger and larger caravans can get in.

In front of the old house was a terrace with a cedar tree, growing alongside the most beautiful stone balustrades. Along here, in past ages, the family had walked, the women in long graceful gowns, twirling their parasols, the men dandified, flirting. There must have been picnics under the cedars, and carriages dashing up to brake opposite the iron-studded oak door, and horses. Kym loved the terrace, but more than that he loved the maze beyond it.

It was a wonderful maze, made of yew, trimmed to perfection. It attracted all the children on the site. They lost themselves inside it, so it had been cut to waist high on an adult. We could find our way and small heads could be seen, and small people rescued, without too many tears.

There were mice in the maze.

We lost Kym, one day when we were in the field close by

the house. He vanished completely. We searched, endlessly, sure he had been stolen. He was such a splendid cat, though I felt that anyone who did take him might soon regret the impulse, as he didn't like strangers, and he was quite capable of biting anyone who handled him against his will. Casey does too, (my present Siamese).

I then realised Kym didn't trust strangers and would hide, which made the search all the more difficult. Also, the place is immense, if you are looking for an object as small as a cat.

Then, I heard his voice. Soft, intrigued, almost amused, coming from the maze. I couldn't see him. I wandered up and down the alleys, calling him, and he answered so that I could pinpoint him, but I could not reach him. There were so many blind ends, and I didn't know where he was. Children adored the maze, as it gave them hours of hunting for one another, crawling so that they did not lose the fun of finding the right way into the centre, playing hide and seek and He.

I found him at last, inevitably by a hole. It wasn't a very interesting hole. To me, at least, it couldn't have sheltered even a mouse whisker, but Kym was sure it held delight. I bent down beside him, as he refused to come with me. He was watching something inside the hole.

I peered in, to a mossy cave, big enough for a fairy about a millimetre high, and there was a beetle; a very splendid, very small beetle, with an electric blue shell and gauze wings and black antennae that wiggled. It may have been a very scared beetle. I didn't know.

'Waugh,' Kym said, very angrily, as I lifted him, and carried him home. After that, whenever we lost him, we found him in the maze.

He would hate Plas Coch now, as it is tidy and the maze has been replaced by a swimming pool and all the old world charm has gone. It's just another site, although it's very well run. Before, it was unique.

Chapter 9

Plas Coch became one of our more regular weekend places, and Kym recognised it as soon as we turned in through the big gates that were flanked by stone pillars. We turned into the drive, where rhododendrons flamed red in May, with bluebells underneath them, with primroses and windflowers in the early spring, with wild garlic everywhere later on, its bitter scent overpowering.

Kym sat on my knee, exclaiming even more loudly. He always exclaimed on the journey, whether in horror or interest we never knew. Travelling with him was a constant entertainment, though the driver wasn't always so amused as Kym could be very trying.

'Waugh,' he shouted, as we went fast along a winding road, with him slipping and sliding, anchoring his claws in our legs. He needed brakes, and used the only ones he had to prevent himself being spilled on the floor as he never learned to balance in the car.

'Waugh,' he yelled as we went over a bridge across the new motorway and he Saw Cars Down There. He couldn't believe it. Down there! He stared and he grew long and thin and his curious head butted against the window. He leaped to the back windowsill to see better. Cars down there. It really was extraordinary and he never got used to that either, repeating his amazement every time we went over that particular flyover, which is above the M6, near Knutsford.

'Waow,' he called softly as we stopped at a crossing, making the policeman on point duty jump and stare to find out just which car had produced such a sinister noise.

Wide-eyed he'd look up at authority, confident that his beauty would cause some comment. It often did.

He even learned that when we stopped, he had to use his earth box, which was kept in the boot, as we didn't want to make a special stop because he was uncomfortable. He let us know that too, pacing and complaining until we recognised his need. A peat box was a vital part of our luggage, and he knew as soon as it was packed that he was coming too.

He kept up a very angry noise until we had passed the five mile limit. The vet's surgery was five miles away. Once he was sure his journey wouldn't end in an injection he relaxed. He was very good about injections, enduring them with only an irritated wail, but he didn't like them. He never again tried to scratch and was one of my vet's favourite patients, as he was so good about any treatment. He would endure patiently even when abscesses were cleaned. I always held him and soothed him and so long as I reassured him he obviously felt safe.

He recognised the caravan site. He exclaimed impatiently as we drove along the avenue, past the little shop, where he was as well known as I was, and down to our site either in the big field on the right, or in the far field by the orchard.

I preferred the orchard site, as there were cattle or sheep beside me every weekend, and I had endless hours of entertainment watching them: picking out the boss, seeing the lambs play, leaving their mothers every afternoon without fail on the dot of four to romp together for an hour. At five the mothers were restless, baaing loudly, and junior felt hungry, and there was a great toing and froing and calling and crying until every ewe had her lamb again, happily sucking, his small tail wagging ardently. The goings-on interested Kym as much as they did me.

Sheep weren't as daunting as cattle, but he didn't like being isolated by them. He became used to them at Plas

Coch, and so when we went instead, one holiday, to St David's Head in Pembrokeshire where we stayed on a delightful farm near the lighthouse, he grew very bold and walked out even though there were sheep about.

It was an extra interesting field, as there were also moles. One was burrowing close to the surface at an unbelievable pace. Kym followed the earthworks, watching the strange movement under the grass, forgetting the sheep.

The ripple in the ground stopped, the mole presumably having gone deep. Kym remembered food. He was always ferociously hungry at the seaside, and so were the rest of us. He turned to come home.

Home was the caravan, right the other side of the fields, and there between him and us was a whole flock of sheep, grazing quietly as it was time to feed just here, and nowhere else. They had been moving purposefully towards us all morning.

Sheep between Kym and us.

He sat, staring at them. He jumped to the top of the gate, and shouted. We were eating and he was safe enough and showed no sign of moving, though he did become more and more agitated. Then with a tremendous burst of courage he decided to come to us, at top speed, as if there were devils at his heels.

The sheep stared.

There was an animal, such as they had never seen before, coming towards them with all the speed and precision of a sheepdog. Kym had been careful not to meet them before. Dogs meant trouble and they didn't know what this was, or what it meant. They flocked together, bleating wildly. Kym, even more alarmed by the noise, came on, trying to dodge round them. They turned in front of him, and he apparently drove them, with the sheep always turning as he turned, keeping between him and sanctuary.

At last he managed to run them away from the van, and raced to us, yelling loudly about his terrible adventure. We were helpless with laughter, which made him even angrier, so that he spent the afternoon sitting, very indignantly, in the shelf by the window, his tail swishing to and fro, while he told the sheep exactly what he thought of them and of us, and of everything else that crossed his mind.

He never was sure what he would find on a caravan site.

He became bolder at Plas Coch, and began to explore. I wasn't very happy about this, as there were hazards, among which were boys with airguns who shot hen pheasants with chicks, and shot rabbits and hares, illegally. My cat, with his dark back and creamy sides, when in long grass might well be mistaken for a rabbit. Friends of mine only recently had had their pet cat mistaken for a rabbit, and shot by a syndicate member on Christmas Day. They found her dead in the garden just before dinner. It was not a pleasant Christmas. And it was not an imaginary hazard.

One Easter, I heard the pheasants in the wood. The male had an alarm call that woke the deaf; his wild yell clamoured in the dawn and I thought perhaps a fox was passing by. A moment later Kym exclaimed loudly as someone began hammering.

Hammer hammer. Hammer hammer.

It was quite impossible to sleep. I dressed, put Kym on his lead and went out into the early morning. We crept into the wood. Kym for once was quiet. The hammering went on, coming, not from the direction of the house, but from the direction of the wood.

'Yow,' Kym said, staring up above my head.

And then I saw the source of the noise. It was a lesser woodpecker, pecking away, so intent on what he was doing that he neither saw nor heard us, but went right on with his din. Further away a louder din began as a greater woodpecker added his noise. I looked for his red cap and saw the flash at the other side of the wood.

I heard the soft croon of a hen pheasant, calling to her chicks. It came from almost under my feet, but I didn't know where. That meant that Kym's explorations must end as I didn't want him to add pheasant chicks to his catches. He had already brought me dead moles that he obviously didn't know what to do with; and any number of shrews, which he never ate after the first time, as that made him very sick. He learned quickly. Shrews have a poison inside them which protects them against predators. Wild cats teach their young that these are unsafe to eat, but no one had taught Kym. He had to learn the hard way. He ate the mice he found. There were so many around us all the time, and he could never resist them, even if he had just fed. Sometimes they disagreed with him too, which was the only evidence I ever had of this particular habit.

But he wasn't having pheasant.

I had already spent some time frightening the cock away from the vans that fed him, after seeing the lads with two dead hen pheasants. The only result of tameness today is that the animal falls victim to ruthlessness. There are too many idiots willing to shoot a sitting hen. So we all stamped and clapped and drove the cock away, much as we would have liked to feed him and hand call him. We weren't popular as other people didn't seem to understand that they were doing harm by gentling the birds. No beast must ever trust man. It's fatal. Only those to whom he belongs, if tame. Dogs and cats can be stolen. One of our Northern Alsatians was stolen at a show this year. I don't like any animal to be overfriendly.

So Kym went back on his lead, but one morning he eluded me and fled out of the door and into the wood.

Something must have chased him, as I couldn't find him anywhere though I could hear him, quite a distance away. I had spent hours in that wood without him, trying to find the hen and her babies, sitting as close as a deer in cover against the trunk of a tree in the shadow, wearing green or brown and trying not to have scent from soap or perfume on me; but I must have smelled of cat, as they never came out.

Now I wasn't thinking of pheasant at all. I was trying to track the sounds Kym was making. They were no longer exclamatory, as when he saw things that intrigued him. They were frantic, as if he were in danger. The wood was a mass of undergrowth, knee high to me, and the grass and nettles and brambles covered the cat so that he couldn't see where he was going. If he couldn't backtrack he might get further and further away and become completely lost.

I plunged through the wood, making enough noise to frighten all the birds for miles. Suddenly, from under my feet, a hen pheasant exploded, taking to the air, and for a few seconds I saw a scatter of tiny chicks, long-legged, yellow-bodied, each with three black zebra stripes down the back. The hen had vanished. And then, so did the babies. I knew they were near me. I had seen them and they hadn't been running. Each had frozen against the ground, still as death, and I couldn't see one of them, try as I looked.

I walked gingerly, afraid I might trample one. Kym was getting desperate. I found him perched on a tree trunk above a dense thicket of stinging nettles. He had gone through them one way and he wasn't coming back. I had no option but to march through to get him. I was partly protected by slacks, but I was wearing sandals and the nettles were powerful.

We walked back through an angry wood, the birds shrieking at us, the cock pheasant, somewhere unseen, setting up his cry of doom. There was no sign of the hen pheasant, but later that night when I went outside the van to look at the sky, bright with stars and a thin crescent moon, I could hear her softly crooning in utter contentment, bedded down, not very far away, with her babies.

By now we had formed a pattern that included the cat, so that he came with us even on long holidays. He was sometimes a nuisance, but more often a source of fun, or of adventure, and once he was the cause of total panic.

We were in Scotland this time, one Whit holiday. Children in the north get a week off school, so we split our summer holiday into two. We were in a field on our own, beside a loch, and we had recently acquired a fibreglass dinghy and taken up fishing. I wasn't sure about the fishing, as I don't like the rocking movement of boats and I much prefer being on shore. I went with the family, feeling it my duty, and endured being cold, feeling slightly sick, and putting worms on hooks and catching fish, though someone else had to kill them for me. I never did feel happy about the process, much as I enjoyed the sea trout that we used to catch, and the excitement when we did catch something. It was a rare event. None of us is good at fishing, which is just as well for my peculiar conscience.

We had left Kym in the caravan safely locked up, as the farmer on whose land we were parked had warned us that there was a killer collie around. They had been hunting him for weeks, going out with guns when they went to look over the sheep, but he was wily, and he was fast, and as soon as they pinned him in one area he changed his ground.

He was a true working collie, gone rotten, from a farm over the hill. Probably a brain tumour, our farmer thought, but no one knows for sure what turns a herder to a killer, and farmers don't have money to spend on post mortems unless something appalling is suspected. This fellow was a big one, and very tough, and we were warned to have no truck with him as he'd turn on us as soon as kill a sheep. He'd already bitten one man. There is no worse killer than a rogue sheepdog. Also he can watch the sheep and single out his prey.

We were fishing when a storm blew up. The wind streaked out of the hills, tossing the waves into rolling white-topped mountains up which we struggled painfully, as we had only a small outboard, sliding into the troughs, the sea deep green and cold beneath us. It seemed to take hours to get to the shore, and I was scared stiff, even if the rest of the family weren't. I probably had more cause as they are all first class swimmers, thinking nothing of diving into the deep sea off a boat, while I loathe cold water. My swimming is just enough to get me across the baths. I also detest being out of my depth.

At last the shore loomed near, and there, to our utter horror, on the beach, was the killer dog, with something black and white in his mouth, tearing away at bleeding flesh. It was very small and it looked like a Siamese cat.

Everyone thought the same.

My husband, for some reason unknown, decided he would be quicker if he jumped into the water, probably because any action seemed better than none. He landed up to his armpits, fully dressed, while we took the boat in. Not deterred by immersion fully clothed, he bent under the water and came up with a handful of very large stones, which he flung.

The dog whipped away, over the wall, leaving his kill behind.

We reached the shore.

I didn't want to look. No one wanted to look. Whatever he had had, had no chance. The body was horribly mauled. My husband walked over.

It was a blackfaced lamb.

It was very dead.

Kym greeted us with glee, safely inside the caravan, purring around us, rolling to have his tummy rubbed, jumping into my arms, looking into my eyes, telling us how lonely he'd been and how long we'd been away and probably how this horrible animal had come to the van and then started to tear up a lamb right under his nose.

He had never been greeted with such fervour by us before. That night as well as his normal food, and the cream tin, he was given a spoonful of cream, which he ate with an expression of dreamy disbelief on his face, and then spent endless moments cleaning his whiskers, savouring every last minute trace.

Chapter 10

Another of our most memorable holidays with Kym was also in Scotland. It was memorable in a number of ways, one of them being the weather, as we were away for twenty-two days, and of those only three were fine.

We started inauspiciously, as it rained all the way from home. It rained on the caravan site where we stayed in the night, and in the morning our elder son contrived to break his glasses, which was a difficult disaster as he can't see without them. They were mended with sticky tape, and we carried on, to fish the next day, and discover when we had packed up our gear that the diamond from my engagement ring had fallen out, and must now be deep under the water.

The next day, just to improve matters, the spring from the clutch of the Land Rover flew up and landed in my lap. I wasn't driving. I fielded it neatly and stared at it, wondering what on earth it was and where it had come from, and found out in the next second.

Repairs effected, we spent the night in a field by yet another loch. Kym went exploring and I found him totally engrossed, patting at a round ball of grass that lay on the ground. Intrigued, I parted the stems. There inside was a minute mouse with five blind babies. She stared up at me, appalled, as she suckled them.

Knowing her terror, I hastily grabbed the cat and went back to the van. By now we had a companion in another van, with a poodle. He also found the nest. The mother was missing this time, and as soon as his owners discovered what it was, they too put their dog on a lead to keep him away from the nursery.

Next day Kym eluded me and went back, and the poodle, leashed, pulled towards the cat and sniffed under his tail. Kym turned round, boxed poodle's ears thoroughly making him squeal, and went back to staring, round-eyed at the grass ball.

He patted it and it fell open. It was empty. I put my hand down. The moss and sheep's wool with which it was lined was still warm. There was no sign of blood, or of disaster. The mother must have made a new nest and removed her babies to safety. All that extra work – life in the wild is merciless.

We had been enchanted by the babies; less than half an inch long, with minute pink noses and tails, and infinitely small claws; and I had been intrigued by the tiny mother, totally engrossed in her small world, living a life that I found hard even to imagine. A life where a giantess could lean down and stare at her with eyes bigger than one of her babies.

We made friends with the poodle's owners, and shared meals, and spent two of the pleasantest days of that particular holiday. We moved on, and on the next site Kym found a slowworm. I had mislaid him again, and heard his intense murmur of delight come from somewhere near a drystone wall.

He was playing with what appeared to be a wriggling piece of thick string. I looked and saw another piece of 'string' moving away from him, stealing between the grasses to slide unnoticed by him into a crevice in the wall. Then I remembered that this beast, which is a legless lizard, can shed its tail and leave it behind, wriggling for long minutes as if still a live reptile, while the rest of the creature escapes. I had never seen a whole slowworm and still never have. Kym played with the tail till it gave up moving over half an hour later, and then came home to have his tea.

That night wildcats fought around us, and he spent the

time at the bottom of my sleeping bag, shivering with fright. I evicted him six times, as he was a very hot companion, but it was futile. He came back immediately.

In the morning, I put him on his lead and walked him, and saw a deep depression in the bracken, with reddish hairs around it, that scared the cat silly. A deer must have lain there. Further on were kills, where the cats had been hunting and had fed. Kym wouldn't walk there at all. He clung demented to my shoulder and yelled and refused after that to go outside the van on his own. Once I saw a tabby back vanish in the shadows. Wild cats are very timid, unless directly attacked. Most wild beasts prefer to run – stupid humans cause the accidents by their own panic behaviour.

Later that day the weather picked up and we decided to move to Loch Leven, and there, while I sat beside the loch, Kenneth and the children decided to climb the mountainside.

I sat on the wall and looked at the water and watched birds flying around me. There was sun on the heather and it was very peaceful. There wasn't a soul about. I might have been alone in the world, and the world new made, without towns or villages to show where man had been. Kym curled up on the wall beside me, glorying in the sunshine. He purred and I felt that if I could purr, I would too.

A small red car flashed into sight, travelling fast.

It passed me, stopped with a scream of brakes and reversed. I watched it approach and out came three large men. Dressed in check shirts and casual trousers; black haired, dark faced, dark eyed, and walking towards me with what I was sure was menace in their movements. I am only five foot two and slightly built and the men looked large.

There wasn't a sign of husband or children.

There wasn't another car on the road.

We had all our money in the Land Rover.

Kym yowled.

The men came on. I sat, not knowing what else to do. Suppose they robbed me? Or raped me? Or killed me? I felt anything but brave.

One of them bowed.

Bowed?

I stared at them, totally astounded.

The other two bowed, and then, very gently, the first one reached out his hand and stroked the cat.

'Bello, bello, bello,' he said.

So they were Italian, and my Italian was precisely nil. One of them had a camera. He pointed it at Kym and said 'please?'

I nodded. There didn't seem much point in saying no as I wasn't at all sure of their intentions and it was very lonely. Perhaps the family would come back soon, but I still might have been all alone in the world, except, now, for three Italians and a small red car.

One of the men took the cat from me.

So they were going to steal him. They were very big men. They looked very determined men.

I sat, like a zombie, feeling sick.

The man holding Kym sat on the wall, and laughed. He had his photograph taken. He handed Kym to the second man, who had his photograph taken, and then he took the camera and the camera man took the cat and he had *his* photograph taken.

One of the men leaned forward and looked into the cat's eyes.

'*Stravigo*,' he said excitedly. '*Stravigo. Stravigo.*'

I stared at him and he put a finger to each eye and crossed his fingers.

'Squint,' I said.

There was a roar of laughter and all three tried to say it.

'Squeent. Squeent. Squeent.'

'What ees?' one of the men said, embracing the whole cat

with a remarkably explicit gesture.

'Siamese,' I said.

They tried to say that too. At this point the family came over the crest of the hill, and saw me, surrounded by three huge men, all apparently on top of me. They pelted down that hill like lunatics, arriving out of breath, Kenneth looking angry.

They found us all helpless with laughter while the men tried to say 'Squint. Siamese' and I echoed with '*Stravigo,*' which for my money I managed a lot better than they did the weird English words.

They bowed to the family, grinned broadly, showed my husband the camera, stroked the cat again and said '*Bello, bello, bello,*' all over again, and drove off, leaving me wondering just where on earth our photographs would land. It still amuses me to think that somewhere in Italy is a picture of an unknown woman and a Siamese cat, both sitting on the wall at Loch Leven side.

My husband seemed to think I should have got into the car and locked it up, which hadn't occurred to me. In any case they were between me and the Land Rover. And it didn't seem wise to show panic. As it happened they were perfectly innocent and very well intentioned, and it was an encounter I wouldn't have missed for all the world.

The sun continued to shine.

The sky was blue and the loch deep green, and the day was perfect.

Until the tow bar broke. The tow bar proved to have pulled out from the metal plate which anchored it on the caravan, so that we had to wait until we could get a repair effected.

We had come to Scotland for peace, and so far had not been able to enjoy it. We had camped beside a loch where wildcats screamed and fought all night; we had camped in a remote part of Argyllshire, where Kym decided to mountaineer and I, hating heights, was the one to get him as no

113

one else thought him in danger. I knew Kym. If he could get into trouble he would.

I climbed perilously over scree and boulder, and came down holding a yelling cat, to find a man with two pointers and a gun telling us we had better move as it wasn't safe where we were. The sea seemed innocent enough and the mountains were far away, but that gun was sufficient to persuade us we were not wanted so we moved on.

Moving on became part of that holiday, as in every place something happened to cause us to seek sanctuary elsewhere. This time we had little choice. We found a camp site beside a pretty loch and settled there, with Fort William only four miles away, and a garage to repair the tow bar within easy distance.

It should have been idyllic but it wasn't, as Prince Philip had very thoughtlessly decided to take his holiday at the same time as ours. He was sailing with the two elder royal children on their yacht, along the Crinan canal. The British public, with its love of royalty, had come in hordes to gawp at them.

We did not want to gawp. We wanted quiet, and rest, and felt that the royal family probably wanted the same, and it was most thoughtless to turn them into a circus.

So wherever we went there were crowds of people and files of cars, usually moving in the opposite direction, turning across us, making what had been planned as a quiet holiday into a nightmare of crowds.

The quiet road beside the loch was far too busy. It was narrow, and we thought led nowhere, but it turned into a race track, and people came fast along it in order to see the Royal Family. We planned not to leave the site, but a phone call revealed that the repair shop wanted cash, and not a cheque. We had to get money.

We shut Kym safely in the caravan. There were super mice in that field and he was longing for freedom. But the cars flashed by all the time, fast. And there were fields on the other side of the road and our cat had a yen for adventure. He also knew the mice were always bigger somewhere else. There were no wildcats here to worry him.

We shut all the windows.

We managed to get our money but the traffic was terrible and we took ages to get back. I opened the caravan door and called.

No cat.

Only the ventilator, that we thought too small for him to get through, was wide open.

We searched the field.

Then I heard a small forlorn cry, coming from a huge clump of bracken. I went over to it and coaxed him.

'Kym.'

The cry was repeated. My cat crawled slowly out of the bracken, his hind leg dragging along the ground, dark with blood that welled from two wounds in his thigh through which protruded two jagged bone splinters.

We were appalled.

I lifted him. He cried forlornly, all the way to the van. I laid him on a newspaper and looked at the leg. It was obviously smashed. How, we didn't know. There were horses and cattle in the adjacent fields. There were cars flashing by non-stop on the roads. Perhaps some car had hit him and the driver had put him safely over the fence. If he had streaked out into the road no driver would have had a chance of avoiding him.

I cursed myself for not having shut the ventilator, but it's too easy to be wise after an event and it makes no odds. What's done is done and no amount of wishing will undo it again. What was necessary now was to find a vet.

We put Kym on newspaper on a large tray and went to find a telephone. The vet would see us. He lived at the edge of the town in a house called Tigh nam Bhet. We thought this meant House of Beasts, but found later it is Gaelic for the Vet's house. I preferred my own translation!

We drove back to Fort William.

It was high noon and very hot and crowds seethed in the streets. We parked the car. Miles from the vet's house. There was no way of getting a vehicle through. I wished heartily that Prince Philip had chosen to go to Bermuda. Or the Canaries. Or anywhere else in the world except Fort William on that day. However, there he was, and there were the sightseers and there was the Press. In force, complaining because it was unpopular. It was equally unpopular with us as its cars got in our way.

I walked through the town holding a crying cat, his leg padded with bloodsoaked tissues. Behind me, grim-faced, stalked the three men of the family. Behind them, bringing up the rear, occasionally sobbing uncontrollably, came our daughter.

There being no royalty to stare at just there, we got stared at instead, astounded faces taking in what must have looked remarkably like an eccentric funeral cortège as by now Kym was only semi-conscious. The black blood was still welling ominously, though slowly. At least no artery was involved.

The vet was Scottish and charming, but he was a large animal vet and he hadn't really the facilities to deal with a cat emergency. He gave Kym a shot of antibiotic and a sedative, confirmed our opinion that he had a broken leg, and said the only thing to do was to take him to Glasgow in the morning, to the Royal Veterinary College at Bearsden, where they could X-ray, and could operate if possible, and also kennel him to nurse him, as obviously we couldn't do it in a caravan; and we didn't want to take him nearly three hundred miles in that state.

It seemed doubtful whether he would survive.

We thrust our way through the crowds and drove back to the site. The tow bar had been repaired but that no longer mattered much. We made a meal, but no one felt like eating. We watched the cat, lying quietly in a cardboard box that the vet had provided.

'Whatever you do, don't let him move,' he had said, as we left.

Later that night we went to bed, with the box on the floor beside our bunk. It was very quiet and very dark. The children fell asleep. I lay and listened to the stertorous breathing that came from the box.

And then came the most extraordinary sound, of slithering and sliding and panting and puffing.

Kenneth got up and lit the calor gas burner.

Kym had climbed out of the box and, fiercely determined, was doing his best to climb up the blanket that covered us. He wanted comfort. He wanted affection. He wanted me.

I padded myself with towels and tissues as the bleeding had started again. It was useless trying to keep him in the box, as once he had made his mind up, obviously not even a broken leg would stop him from trying to gain his objective. It was his right hind leg. It hung there, horribly, as if it didn't belong. He was lifted and put gently into my arms. He licked my hand and settled, staring at nothing, quiet now that he felt safe.

We drank tea all night, as I dared not sleep in case I turned over and harmed him even more by shifting his leg further out of position. The vet had tried to put it in the right place but it did not stay there. He thought the head of the femur, the big thigh bone, had been completely shattered.

It began to rain.

Rain beating on the caravan roof, and drumming on the ground.

We drank more tea. The children woke up. The rain went on, and the cat lay quiet, just so long as I held him. As soon as we put him in the box, he tried to get back to me.

There was nothing for it but to nurse him.

We had to go back to the vet at seven for a tranquilliser

before our journey. We were dressed by five. The hours passed endlessly. We reached the vet's house at seven o'clock on the dot. He was obviously not yet awake, as he arrived, very sleepily, in his pyjamas, to give the necessary injection, and then gave us directions for our journey.

By now it was raining as only in Scotland can it rain.

Rain on the roads. Rain beating on the roof. Rain on the windscreen, so torrential that sometimes it ran up instead of down and the wipers could not control it.

There was no scenery. The mountains had vanished. The road was reduced to a few yards of track. Rain hid everything from us. The day was as bleak as our mood, and Kym reacted badly to the tranquilliser and went slightly crazy.

He yowled, long and loud and eerily.

He chewed away half of the cardboard box and then struggled out of it on to my lap, where he alternated biting my hand with biting the upholstery of the seat.

It turned into a nightmare journey. Nothing would quieten him. Every time he moved blood welled out again from the two deep holes. Horrible thick blackish blood, that soaked the tissues.

At last we reached Glasgow.

Our directions did not appear to lead us to Bearsden. We asked the way.

Inevitably the first passerby was a total stranger to the town. The second was a very old man with no teeth and such a strong accent we could only surmise that he was actually speaking in a tongue we ought to have understood.

The third passerby directed us.

We drove into the college park, and up to the entrance. I walked inside, holding a cat that by now was nearly out of his mind. So was I.

Quiet competent men took him from me, and we went to the X-ray room. I waited, holding Kym, until they came back with the plates. The head of the femur had been sheared right off the shank; and the shank was splintered.

'What can you do?' I said. Kym was only four and I didn't want him put down.

They shrugged.

'There's nothing we can do. There's nothing to pin. Time will heal the break, but he will always be very lame. It's up to you.'

'Can you keep him here and nurse him? We can't really keep him quiet in the caravan.'

That was the easiest part of it. I was warned that once the tranquilliser wore off he would be suffering from delayed shock. He might die on them. I didn't want him to die among strangers, but if we travelled him any more, he hadn't a chance. And these, after all, were experts.

We left him, arranging to phone every day at 11 a.m. for a report, as they thought we would want to know how he was progressing and also, if anything did transpire, we might be able to help them cope with him, as Siamese are notorious for being awkward individualists whose routine must go on no matter if the skies fall in.

We drove back through the rain and the dark to a washed-out camp site, and an empty caravan. We burned the box and the tissues and decided to stay put and fish as once the Royal yacht had travelled on, it would be peaceful again.

I rang daily at eleven.

Kym was alive, but he wasn't eating, though he would take glucose and water. They held out little hope.

On the Sunday when I rang, he hadn't eaten for four days. It was, they thought, the end of the line. I was about to ring off when I suddenly had an idea.

'What are you feeding him?'

They told me. It was one of the proprietary catfoods, lauded always on television, the delight of all cats. Except mine. He would rather starve than eat it and had never ever touched the stuff. He sniffed it, scratched the floor disgustedly with his hind legs and yelled for proper food.

'What does he like ?'

'He adores plaice,' I said. 'And cod, at a pinch.'

I went back to report. We spent a dismal day, reading and eating, as it was still very wet. We shopped, and came back to the silent van. Kym had been part of it for so long that we couldn't bear it without him to greet us and even missed his constant yells while we were driving.

I rang next day, expecting to hear that my cat was dead.

'I went down to the docks', the voice said. 'I got him fish straight out of the sea, as the boats came in. He's eating like a tiger.'

It was all I could do to thank her. I went back to report and we spent a much happier day, sure our cat had turned the corner. We were due to go home the following weekend, taking two days over the drive. Would Kym be fit to travel?

'Yes', they said, next day.

The skies were clearing as we drove back to Glasgow. This time we could even see Glencoe, which had been invisible in the mist before. It was rain-soaked still and gloomy, the mountains brooding around the road, but its atmosphere did not affect us this time. We were going to get Kym and were going home and surely next year's holiday couldn't be as bad as this? There was always tomorrow.

We found the college easily this time. I jumped out of the car and went inside.

'We'll miss Kym', one of the vets said. 'He's quite a lad.'

He sent a girl to fetch him and I watched a horse being led up and down, in an attempt to diagnose the source of its lameness. Our younger son was with me, enthralled by everything he saw. We waited, neither of us aware that eight years later he himself would be one of the men in white coats, studying to be a vet at Glasgow. He qualified some years ago and I often wonder if he remembers his fascination that day, and if that is what led to his final choice of a career. All because of a cat.

'I wonder what Kym will make of us, after a week?' I said

idly, knowing my cat. When I came home from a month in America he ignored me for four days after the initial greeting, apparently to teach me not to go away and leave him again. He might well do the same this time.

He was within hearing distance of my voice. He recognised it, and the yell he let out produced a roar of laughter.

'That's your Kym,' someone said.

He was in his kennel girl's arms, but as soon as he saw me he reached out towards me though he was yards away, pawing frantically, begging me to come and take him, shouting to me, telling me that he had been away from us for ever and what on earth were we up to and come and get him quick, quick, quick.

He came into my arms, rolling and purring, singing his joy.

'I'm going to miss him,' the nurse said, somewhat tearfully. She patted him, and I paid his bill and we went back to the Land Rover. He greeted everyone with a robust noise that made us forget that his leg still dangled uselessly, although the wounds had begun to heal. The fur had been cut away and there were two deep holes where the bones had come through. I don't know even now what they did about those splintered ends, but assumed they were cut away and the wounds tidied. He certainly hadn't been operated on.

The journey home was a riot. Kym was so excited to be with us again that he commuted from lap to lap, ending up on mine, snuggled against me, washing my hand until it was sore from his rough tongue. He leaned up to look into my face and purred.

We drove on to the Erskine ferry.

People stared at him and he started to tell his story all over again, with emphasis, leaning out of the car window to peer earnestly into faces. The ticket collector couldn't stop laughing at him and when he heard about the broken leg commented he wasn't surprised the cat had so much to say.

We were late getting off, as the man forgot to collect the money for the tickets, and so many people came over to look at the cat with a broken leg that it felt like a royal procession all over again.

Kym shouted to the policeman on point duty in Penrith. He told everybody, at every red traffic light, leaning out of the window, talking so much I was sure he would lose his voice. We didn't care; we were so pleased to have him back that his constant noisy comment was a source of amusement rather than irritation.

It was necessary to hold him very carefully, as he had no sense of balance at all. The loss of the use of his right hind leg had completely upset his ability to keep himself from sliding all over the car.

We reached home. We carried him indoors and set him down. He could lie on one side. He could, with immense difficulty, move on three legs, the hind one dragging. It took him almost a minute to make a step and I began to wonder if I had been wise to keep him alive. A crippled cat could have so little fun.

And then I remembered my broken arm and how long that had taken to heal and how little movement I had had in it for weeks afterwards, yet now, years later, no one would know it ever had been broken. It was only just over a week since Kym was hurt.

He could balance on his earth box if I held him.

His appetite was unimpaired.

So long as he was near me, he was content. He watched everything I did and as usual commented on it. He cried to be carried upstairs when I went to make beds, do bedrooms, sort clothes. He came down again into his box in the kitchen while I worked there; and the box was at my feet while I typed.

Once more, he was bound to me, as he had been when a kitten; he couldn't go out, except when he was carried.

And he wasn't going to use that leg at all.

Then, one morning, I put him under the window in a patch of sunlight, in our bedroom, while I finished changing sheets. I was on the other side of the room when I heard a soft call.

He was standing up, his weight taken, just for a moment, on his hind leg. He made a small noise that sounded like 'ooh', a swift intake of breath, like an old man with rheumatism, and collapsed on the floor. An hour later, he stood again, just testing that leg, testing its strength, seeing if it would bear any weight.

He did this about ten times a day for nearly a week.

At the end of a week, he walked one step, and dropped. Again, he repeated this, until he was trying to walk his one step several times an hour. Every time he had had enough he dropped, as if he'd been shot, no matter where he was. In the middle of the kitchen or sitting room or hall; or on the lawn, where I took him for fresh air.

Then he began to make progress. First only two steps at a time; then four; then he was limping atrociously, but walking down the hall, very slowly, with extreme difficulty. He could move around downstairs and follow me. The vet, who was keeping a strict eye on his progress, thought it a good idea to let him walk, as animals, unlike humans, don't overdo things. If he felt he'd had enough, he rested. And nothing on earth would shift him until he decided he could bear to do a little more work on that leg.

Then one day, about two months after the accident, I heard the most odd noise on the stairs. Kym had been asleep when I went up. I looked down, and there he was, coming upstairs; one front paw, two front paws, and then a bunny hop, bringing both hind legs up together, in the oddest way. Before his accident he had walked upstairs, one two three four. Or rather, he had raced up. He never walked until he broke his leg.

He was very pleased with his new method of progress and spent the next week hopping upstairs. Very tryingly, as

123

it turned out, since coming down was beyond him and he sat and yelled until I fetched him, at which point, unless I shut us both in, he promptly went up again and yelled to come down again.

Now the vet suggested walks on a lead to strengthen the muscles.

This was fine, but Kym decided lead walks should be in front of the house and *not* at the back. Possibly walking on grass was more difficult than walking on pavement, as he preferred linoleum to carpet for practising in the house.

I didn't mind walking him on the lead until a gang of men came to dig up the road and lay a sewer. The whole road was up and there were about twenty men working. Large men who stared at this incredible sight: a woman with a limping cat that lay down on the path every ten paces, and then at the end of the road had to be carried back.

It was on the first of these sorties that I discovered what really had happened to him.

A car came round the corner while we were out. It was then a fairly quiet road. No two-car families, and few of the women drove. Kym heard the car, turned his head, saw it, and was up into my arms, terrified, trembling, hiding his head in my shoulder, holding on tight with all his claws. After that I picked him up when I heard a car coming, to avoid being scratched in his anxiety to get to safety fast.

He learned later that cars needed avoiding, but he always trusted me and knew the sound of my engine. He used to appal me when I was driving by appearing suddenly from under the hedge, running in front of the car to greet it, knowing I would stop and pick him up and put him inside for safety. I took to making sure he was indoors before I drove out as I was afraid some dark night I might not see him. My next door neighbour had reversed over Dusky one dark morning on Christmas Eve some years before, to everyone's horror, most of all his. He had spent a terrible day hunting for another Persian cat, and now Shady Lady lived next door, timid, tortoiseshell in colour, very beautiful and sure Kym was a devil.

The men watched us daily. Kym needed exercise. He had to get that leg better. He had to learn to balance all over again and held his tail at the oddest angles to get himself in the right position. He had learned to use his left paw to open doors instead of his right, as if he used his right, he promptly fell over. He even learned to chase a string left-pawed. He was a natural right hander.

But he had to think. He would start to move the right paw, consider, and change his mind. He used his head to help him get the door open as it opens the wrong way for a left-pawed cat.

One day, seeing the men look at one another as I appeared yet again, towing my limping Siamese, I smiled at the foreman.

'I'm not mad,' I said. 'He broke his leg and he has to walk to get the muscles strong again.'

The men grouped round us to see him and his leg and hear all about it, mostly from me, but Kym put in a word or two here and there just to make sure we remembered him.

After that we had a regal progress, with everyone watching to see if he were improving, and by the time the men had finished the road repairs they were all firm friends of Kym's and entertained to watch him.

Years later a large workman stopped me in the main village street.

'Have you still got that cat?' he asked.

'Kym? Not now. I have two little blue points now.'

'Did his leg get better?'

I recognised him then. He had been foreman on the road gang all those years before and remembered us and had wondered about us.

One morning soon after the men had gone, I found Kym jumping from one chair to another. Jump. Jump. Jump.

Backwards and forwards again and again.

I couldn't make out why until I saw his tail. He was re-learning to jump, and he needed a different angle on that tail to balance him. He was experimenting, so that he did not make a mistake and suffer for it.

That was the next exercise.

First walking.

Then stairs.

Now jumping.

From chair to chair.

From floor to table.

From floor to sill.

From floor to top of the sideboard.

Up and on and flop.

Up and on and flop, with a loud shout of triumph when he got it right, and a yell to come and see what he was doing and how clever he was.

He still tired very easily. Outdoors was only a short adventure and he came home quickly, knowing perhaps instinctively that he hadn't a chance should he be involved in a fight.

That was the one blissful part of the whole thing.

No fights for nearly a year.

And then came a day when I watched him run down the garden, climb the apple tree, and run back again, using an odd sideways sidle which hid the fact that his right hind leg was now one inch shorter than the other three. You could only see that when he stretched. It didn't reach the floor. No one even guessed when he was walking or running or jumping. They looked at me in disbelief.

Some time later we X-rayed the leg after he had a fall.

He hadn't injured himself that time. There where the broken head met the bone shaft, he had made a whole new joint of callus. And what was more, though the College in Glasgow, the vet in Fort William, and our own vet, had told us he most likely would not have full mobility, he had as usual proved all the experts wrong.

I was very glad indeed that I had not given way to my first impulse to save him suffering, and had him put to sleep. He was in splendid shape again.

Chapter 11

We were learning as well as Kym. Now, when we left the van, the ventilator was shut tight as well as the window. He might not try the trick again, but we were taking no risks. Apart from anything else his adventure was very expensive, what with kennelling in Glasgow for a week, and the X-rays and then all the aftercare from our own vet. No national health for animals. Though sometimes I think they get far better attention than we do, as the vets have more time and far more incentive than the overworked doctors, bound by rules and regulations and forms. I dislike the welfare state intensely. I prefer to stand on my own feet. I'm not a baby in need of constant care.

Adventures were by no means over for Kym. There is always something new in the wild, and our chosen caravan sites were often very wild indeed.

One night, in yet another Scottish field, Kym slipped out into the dusk. I always watched him now, listening to his comments coming from the ripple in the long grass that showed where he walked. He commented non-stop.

He was very funny, as he would keep up a running commentary wherever he was, so that we could pinpoint his whereabouts. Goodness me, what's that? Oh, a monster. *Smell* . . . lovely. You could put words into his mouth, and we often wished we could understand what he was saying.

There was a moon that night; it was full and high and he watched it, sitting absolutely still on a fence post like a formal Egyptian statue, his tail wrapped round his legs, his front legs neatly side by side, his head erect, his ears moving to catch the noises on the wind. One ear forwards, and then another, and then back again, or both suddenly angling towards a noise in the grass.

He had slipped out of the open window. It was very hot that night. There was the beginning of a gale, the wind stroked his fur and he watched the grass blowing, sure it was the trail of a million unseen mice. His eyes followed the movement, but his body was absolutely still. Only his ears were alive. The rest of him might have been petrified.

There were other things in the grass. A feather blew. He crouched. His hind end swayed, again and again and again, and then he pounced and took the feather and began to play, an airy dance, alone under the moon. Up in the air and leap and catch, his body twisting, his movements as controlled and elegant as those of any first class ballet dancer.

There were other creatures out in the dusk. Kym was off guard, not watching, absorbed by his feather. There was a sound on the air, and a shadow on the ground.

He was at the far end of the field and there was nothing we could do. Long ago instincts alerted him. He leaped quietly out of sight into the long grass, where he must have frozen, flat against the ground, his small heart beating wildly.

There was a golden eagle above him.

The bird must have seen him and mistaken him for a rabbit. It had perched on the dead branch of an old tree. Kym lifted his head.

The bird flew towards him.

Kym began to steal towards the caravan, his body barely moving, creeping, long and low, intent on coming. Inch by patient inch, so that the grass scarcely rippled. He leaped to the ditch and I lost sight of him. He was still too far from us to do any good at all. He had wandered further than usual. We were outside, walking towards him, but he couldn't see us and the bird was intent on the shadow in the grass.

Kym came out of the ditch, saw us and ran. He ran hell

for leather, racing towards us, trusting us to rescue him, unaware that we doubted our ability if the bird should swoop and grab him. There was nothing to throw. There was nothing we could do. Nothing at all.

Kym covered the ground unbelievably fast. I was afraid his recently healed leg might betray him, as it was the first time he had run at such speed. He was shadowed by the bird, looming over him, waiting for a chance to position itself so that it could drop and grab. Kym was no bigger than a half-grown hare and probably looked very like one as he raced towards us.

He was within reach. He passed us speeding towards the van and leaped inside, and we followed him and closed the door. He had come so fast his head had hit the wall opposite the door and he was slightly stunned.

There was an immense thump as the bird hit the corner of the caravan. The van shook, and so did the cat. He came to me, jumping into my arms, pushing his head inside my jacket, trying to melt against me, his body rigid and trembling. It was a long time before he left the van again; and it was the last time he went out at night. He had no desire to tangle with the vast winged shadow that had hunted him across the field, and terrified him beyond measure.

Birds in the wild were nothing like birds at home. Often, at Plas Coch, Kym watched the half tame pheasant. He never tried to stalk it. It walked, regal, in the field, its brilliant plumage making it very conspicuous against the grass. If he were outside, he sat, watching, suspicious. Was it a bird? Would it turn on him and rend him? It was enormous. Bigger than he was. We could almost see his brain ticking as he tried to work this out.

But prudence always won, and he came in and watched through the window, where he was eternally brave, chattering his fury noisily, shouting abuse, but never venturing outside to challenge and test his strength against the imperious beauty that walked as if he owned the earth, and that yelled like a demon in the early dawn when the fox came by.

There were other dangers too. He loved to sit by the fence and watch the goings-on in the field. Sometimes there were cattle. On one occasion they rounded the cattle and I put Kym in the van. He watched as I took my place by the gate, having been asked to help.

'Move to the side and head that one off', someone yelled.

Obedient, I moved, and stood like a ninny as the most immense cow I had ever seen cantered towards me. I am used to cows, so stood my ground and said things to it. It skidded to a stop and stood there, while the farmer shut the gate, rather to my surprise, leaving the rest of the herd behind.

He came up to me grinning.

'You've got a nerve', he said, and only then did I look again at the beast that stood facing me, and realised that they had been separating the bull from the herd and I had stood there while he galloped up to me. I had been so sure it was a cow and that I could cope, that I hadn't turned a hair. I pretended nonchalance and watched the monster led off by a halter round his neck. Luckily he was nothing like as fierce as the fellow I met some years later, when on an outside job. That day the photographer I was with was crouched behind one car and I was flat between the wall and another car while men with pitchforks tried to corner the bull, who was sure we would provide him with much more fun than his pen.

I went inside and this time it was Kym who sat on my lap and helped me regain my own nerves, as I suddenly realised what a fool I had been.

Later that day I let Kym out and it was his turn for trouble, as the crows had decided to come and feast on the cattle droppings, not in ones and twos, but in numbers. Kym saw one of them. It was just a bird. He began to stalk.

The sentinel in the tree by the caravan saw him and

shouted.

Crows act in unison.

In no time at all they were on him, flying at him, yelling at him, diving at him, and he was running for his life. This time I had ammunition and he was near. I hurled large stones at the birds but they came on relentlessly. I remembered the kittens I had found in a field when I was a small girl, their eyes pecked out by crows.

I ran towards the birds, yelling like a dervish, getting between them and the cat, flapping my arms in front of my own face, not at all sure that I wouldn't end up like the people in Daphne du Maurier's horrifying story *The Birds*. I had once been dive-bombed by seagulls when I was near their nest and they too had raked at my eyes.

Kym reached the van.

The birds lost interest, but they settled on the fence, staying there like ghouls all the afternoon, watching us with remorseless eyes. If I moved they flapped off, but came back, as if lying in wait.

Neither Kym nor I went out again that afternoon.

The vigil ended at dusk when the crows flew home to roost.

Later that incident and many others formed part of my book *Casey*. Kym always featured if only briefly in every book I wrote, right up to his death. He was part of everything I did, teaching me about wild life, showing me things I might have missed, alerting me to birds and bird calls and their alarm signals. My dogs do it now.

Then Kym discovered frogs. We have frogs at home, goodness knows why, as there isn't any water. These he ignored until one day, beside a loch in Scotland, he came on a frog sitting on the beach.

It leaped away from him. It was a large frog, and of course it immediately attracted his attention. Had it kept still, he might have failed to see it. He stalked it, reached it, and tapped it with an experimental paw. It leaped high in the air, making a shrill squeaking sound that alerted me to its plight.

Kym was some hundred yards away from me, and intent on his game.

Stalk, tap, *squeak*.

Stalk, tap, *squeak*.

I called him, as I don't like torture, but he was much too engrossed to hear.

I ran and picked him up. He was furious and told me so, all the way back to the caravan, complaining loudly because I'd interrupted this wonderful new sport.

After that, he was aware of frogs and the immense possibilities they had for fun. He began to stalk them at home.

The shrill squeal they made was plainly audible. Even when I was upstairs I knew at once what was happening and raced out to stop the game. All the way across the lawn I would see and hear it. Stalk, Pat. Leap and squeak.

Never a croak.

Just a shrill squeal like a squeaky toy. Kym had a squeaky rubber toy and may well have thought this was another, as he had no desire to kill. Only to play.

I later used this incident in *The Running Foxes*, and much to my surprise the reviewer in the *Field* commented that Mrs Stranger had used her fertile imagination and he didn't believe that frogs squeaked. They croaked. I was rather irritated as I had seen and heard it for myself, only too often. It isn't in the least like the natural croak. The same reviewer commented that herons wouldn't change their flight course because of a fox; but herons are part of our lives – herons on the Menai Straits, herons fishing the Scottish lochs, herons staking out their places on the shore – and I have seen them inspect their usual place safely from the air, find it occupied by either our Kym, or a strange dog wandering from the village near by, and immediately change course and fly away.

Many people, among them reviewers, tend to think that

because they have not seen a thing, or read about it in some book, then it doesn't happen. I have never seen a panda. But that doesn't mean I don't believe it exists.

I commented a year or two ago on this particular review to Professor Arthur Cain, who at that time was zoology professor at Manchester University and was a neighbour of ours. He was engaged on a BBC programme on animals. He had also often heard frogs squeak and was as critical of that review as I was.

The frog games went on for the whole of Kym's life. I have only seen a frog once since then, when I nearly chopped one in two with the lawn edge trimmers, and it leaped panic-high and squeaked, and at once I conjured up a picture of a small intent cat stalking across the lawn, paw tapping at the appalled frog, while I ran out to stop his antics and carry him in, with him trying to struggle free and carry on with this wonderful occupation.

Although we did not know it at the time, our last touring holiday in the van was to be another odyssey, all round Scotland. We revisited our favourite places; Loch Creran in Argyllshire, Loch Fyne, the Ardgarten site near Rest and Be Thankful (where we always did and were); and then on to tour more remote regions where we had never been before.

This time we tended to keep Kym in, and he seemed to have less desire for adventure. He was now seven, and though far from staid, was less likely to get into kitten troubles, though right up to the end of his life his curiosity continued to lead him into peculiar situations.

One night, unable to find any site near us, we parked in a small quarry beside the water. That night was a truly Scottish night, with the wind howling in the trees, the waves lashing white against the shore, and the rain beating on the caravan roof, a sound like the drumbeats of doom.

I could not sleep.

Neither could Kym.

Most nights he inhabited a shelf on top of a cupboard beside the window of the van. Here he had his blanket. Here he could look out and watch the night, which always fascinated him. He would sit, absolutely still except for his moving ears, and stare at the stars and the moon; at the wind in the grass and whatever walked out there in the dark. He knew far more about it than I did.

Sometimes there were terrifying creatures abroad and then he vacated his shelf and came to me, snuggling deep inside my sleeping bag. He was heavy and he was hot and I evicted him, but in the end gave up, as he was more determined than I was and far less sleepy.

This night the family slept while the wind shrieked around and the rain lashed against the windows.

'Waugh,' said Kym, and then, in case I hadn't heard, said it again. I could see him in the dimness. He was staring out of the window and then turning to look at me.

Something was out there.

I thought of fox and wildcat and went to look, creeping softly so that I didn't disturb everyone else.

I looked out of the window.

The waves were white against the shore. The bay curved, bounded by a tiny wood, and there in the wood was a spectral figure, robed like a monk, with a cowled head, and an outstretched arm that wavered up and down in the dark, pointing out across the water. It shivered eerily, and it was phosphorescent.

I picked Kym up and crept back into my bunk, hoping the figure would stay where it was and not prowl around the van. I don't believe in ghosts. Well, not really. Only . . . you never know. I thought of waking the family, but that wouldn't achieve anything at all and anyway Kenneth, being a scientist, doesn't believe in ghosts either. And of course, it wasn't really there. It couldn't be.

Kym climbed onto my chest and peered out of the window beside my bunk. 'Waugh,' he said. I grabbed him, and looked out too. It was there. It hadn't moved, and the quivering had increased. Also it seemed to be eight feet high and looking towards us.

I lay back, listening to the wind.

There was a scream. A devil scream, that made Kym shiver and dig his claws into me.

Hunting owl.

Creeping wildcat.

Courting fox.

The scream came again, unearthly, while the wind screeched too and the waves crashed endlessly on the rocks, and the van shook and the darkness was unbroken except, when I sat up and peeped again, for a ghostly figure, eight feet high, with a hooded head and a pointing arm.

I was safe in the van. It didn't seem to want to move.

What doom did it foretell?

Or what horrid deed had been done here that brought that silent haunting shape to stand endlessly beside the wild water? Was it always there?

I remembered Lord Ullin and his erring daughter:

'"Come back, come back," he cried in grief,
Across this stormy water.
And I'll forgive your Highland chief,
My daughter, oh my daughter.'

I couldn't remember all of it but I remembered that when the boat sank,

'one lovely hand was stretched for aid,
And one was round her lover.'

Was Lord Ullin himself doing endless penance? The history of Scotland was wild and as stormy as the night and anything could have happened here. I dozed, and woke, and looked out, to see that eerie figure unmoving, among the trees. Kym was equally restless and equally intrigued, and we looked together. I was very glad of the warmth of his small body and the loud purrs that greeted my stroking hand whenever we dared to lie down again.

The night ended.

The wind dropped.

The rain ceased.

I said nothing to the family.

I put Kym on his lead and carried him, in his usual perch on my shoulder, into the little wood.

The figure, to my horror, was still there, pointing out to sea.

I approached it warily, and then began to laugh. The family found me sitting on a rock, helpless with amusement. My ghost was a shipping marker, a post eight feet tall with a pointing arm and a round notice on top of it, warning of undersea cables. It was phosphorescent so that it would show up at night. The shivering appearance was given by the moving leaves of the trees that partly masked it.

I never confessed my fears, and no one could imagine what was the matter with me as every time I saw the thing that day I was reduced to peals of laughter at the thought of the terrible night I had spent, all for nothing.

I nearly told them three weeks later, at the end of the holiday, when we were again unable to find a site and the post office told us we could camp on the 'wee bit moor'. 'Ye'll no be disturbed,' they added.

The moor was bleak. There was a tiny wood, in which were a few stunted trees, and there were ponies that circled the wood, but never went inside. There were hoof marks everywhere, but nothing there. Nor were there any birds. It was completely silent.

The children went into the wood and came out again.

'I don't like it', one of them said.

By now I had eyes watching me, but when I turned there was no one there. I had an immense uneasiness, an increasing anxiety, and a total dread. I said nothing, knowing it was absurd, but we all went back to the van and spent the evening inside. Kym refused to go out at all and we filled his earth box, with difficulty as it's surprisingly hard to find bare earth in the wild.

I could not sleep.

The van was moonlit and ghosts walked outside. Fear walked beside them. I felt slightly sick. I lay, watching the moon, with Kym tucked in the crook of my arm, wanting to be as close to me as he could get.

Just after midnight Kenneth went outside and came back some minutes later with an immense stick.

'What's that for?' I whispered.

'I don't know. This place is horrible. Shall we go as soon as it's light?'

I couldn't wait for light. Some time before daybreak we made tea. The children were awake too. Light came at last and we couldn't get away fast enough. The feeling of doom didn't leave me all day, but that night we were beside another loch, on the way home, and here the air was fresh and clean and Kym happily came out with me to explore, and we slept well.

Some years later I told a Scottish friend of this experience, and she got out her map.

'Where were you?' she asked.

I pointed.

'No one local would ever go there', she said. 'That was where they massacred the last stragglers from one of the major battles in Prince Charlie's day. It's haunted.'

Haunted it certainly was, by fear and oppression; by unseen shapes, by long-ago terrors. I have never been so sure that ghosts didn't exist since then. I could feel the nightly army, the killers and the slain, enacting their terrible deeds, over and over. The story haunted me until it made its way into a book, *The Fox at Drummer's Darkness*. I had known the eerie feeling of that moor, and somehow, that book wrote itself out of the long-ago past, and my own past, when Kym shuddered in my arms and unseen evil prowled around us all night.

Chapter 12

Life changes all the time. The family were growing up and the boys needed adventure. So did our daughter. So Kenneth, who had always yearned for a boat, as he had boated throughout his boyhood, with one of his uncles, sold the dinghy and bought instead a two-berth Silhouette, a small tub of a yacht that sailed rather like a cow, but that gave plenty of scope for all kinds of adventures.

We also sold the van and bought a larger one, plumbed into the alleyway of permanent caravans at Plas Coch, as I have no love for the sea. It is cold and grey and deep and gruesome, a killer of men, and when I am on it, I am always haunted by the thoughts of what lies far below me, and the fear that I might well join those who have sunk for ever under the waves.

Also, I hate the endless rolling; the necessity of being tied in a small space by tide and wind; the need to study the weather; my inability to escape from the family and walk on the hills and watch the sun on the trees, and the water that broods at the foot of high mountains.

The sea is monotony, an endless boredom, and those who try to convert me are wasting their time. Not that it stops them. So many people seem to think that if a wife doesn't do exactly the same as her husband, she is failing in her duty. We have never seen marriage like that. We are two separate people, both entitled to enjoy our own activities and abilities to the full, not imposing slavery on one another by insisting that one gives up everything for the other, no matter what inclination there might be to do something different. I used to play tennis, to ride whenever there was a stable near, and to walk. The family could boat all they wanted. Sometimes I joined them, but always that splitting headache came back, and the constant queasiness that made me hate the holidays spent on the water, and long for dry land and changing scenery and colour.

The family all loved the boat, so I bought myself a car of my own and explored while they sailed. I sat beside each one in turn while he or she learned to drive, exploring the whole of Anglesey. I slept in the van with Kym, and explored the site with him, and relaxed and read all the books I hadn't had time to read.

I travelled, as no one else wanted to travel, and went to America for a month, while the family looked after Kym. He spent the month on my bed, rarely going outside, never coming downstairs. The night my boat docked at Liverpool he came downstairs and sat on the windowsill. He was still sitting there when I came home. He greeted me ecstatically, rolling and purring, and then ignored me, to teach me not to leave him as he objected.

I went to Ireland for my holidays, which I spent in a nature reserve run by friends of mine. Clare and Fred have moved now to a smaller place, but Garnafailagh remains one of my favourite holiday places. It was the background for *The Honeywell Badger*, for there I sat in trees and listened to the night while badgers and foxes roamed beneath me and sometimes fought.

Kym became a boating cat.

Sometimes I went out with them for the day, and Kym then very firmly anchored himself to me. He didn't really know what to do when the boat heeled, as his need was always to be high. He never did learn to go with the boat, but at each tack, as the bunks changed position, so did he. He clung for dear life to the canvas bench backs, convinced he was much safer up there, like a limpet on rock, than comfortably lying down with the boat lifting above him. It kept him very active.

142

So it was a relief to have me there too, wearing a zipped anorak into which he could crawl, only his head sticking out under my chin.

He travelled out to the boat in a sack, as he hated the look of the sea close to him and yelled if it splashed him, as it invariably did. If I were there, being splashed too, he could shelter under my oilskins, but the family preferred not to wear him. He was apt to use his claws if he felt unsafe, sticking them firmly into our legs or arms to make sure he was safe, never mind the rest of the world.

Then the family prevailed on me to try boating. The children were positive I'd never really given it a chance. 'You'll love it,' they insisted, not believing that anyone could fail to enjoy being marooned at sea in a high wind with the boat bouncing like a dancing doll, riding up the waves and sliding down the waves, on and on, on and on, in an eternity that seemed to have no boundary.

I have never decided whether my hell will be to be incarcerated for ever in a small boat on a grey sea with no chance of getting ashore, or driving up a motorway in pelting rain, while giant lorries shower rear window, windscreen and mirrors with mud and I can't find an exit. There are hells on earth; I hope there are none in eternity.

My paradise is a grassy field, with cowslips, and mares and foals galloping, and my cats and dogs beside me. There I could live for ever and want nothing else, so long as the summer sun shone.

Meanwhile, I promised to try the boat, properly, not half-heartedly, not begrudgingly. I was married to a dedicated sailor and perhaps I had better become dedicated too. After all many women loved it. They came to the boat club and tried to reform me, telling me I didn't know what I was missing, that I would revel in it once I decided to enjoy it and not loathe it, that there was so much scope for all kinds of unusual things, like balancing on an elsan when the boat is leaping around like a six month colt, and having

143

to get ashore through deep mud that clings to the legs and sucks off Wellingtons, and not being able to shop until the tide has turned, and there isn't any food aboard that's worth eating, as the bread is stale and the vegetables seem to have become soaked in sea water from that wave that drenched everyone and left our clothes remarkably damp and undryable as there isn't anywhere to dry them.

But I tried.

Dear heaven, how I tried. I tried for four years, during which my only consolation was that Kym felt more or less the way I did. When the helicopter came over, and dived to look at the odd animal sunbathing on the deck, he fled into the chain locker and refused to come out.

When one of the boys dived into deep water off the side of the boat, and showered us all, he fled under a bunk, swearing and refused to come out.

When I, being a fool, not knowing when I had been punished enough, slept aboard, listening all night to creaks and groans and the slap slap slap of water on the sides, Kym inspected the boat before bed and then, with a deep sigh, curled up beside me. This was even less comfortable than in the caravan as the bunk was a narrow prison, and he kept slipping so had to use his claws.

When I went ashore, Kym rode me. In my lap in the boat; on my shoulder all the way to the van. Cold, wet, slightly sick and unable to balance, I staggered up the hill, with Kym bawling his head off, whether because he was so thankful to be ashore or because he was uncomfortable, being by now too big for my shoulder, so that I needed one hand to help him balance. It was useless putting him down as he wouldn't walk, and simply climbed me again . . . and again . . . and again.

You can never dissuade a Siamese cat. One of our present pair thinks he is a bird and serenades us at dawn. Complain and he is quiet for exactly one minute before he starts off again.

Kym was even more persistent. Had he wanted to call us at dawn, he wouldn't have stopped at all. He would have gone right on yelling. Luckily that wasn't one of his habits. He was quiet until we woke up.

We exchanged the Silhouette for a Gallant which was four-berth. Everyone was sure I would love it as it was bigger and therefore more comfortable. Unfortunately *Shona* thought she was a corkscrew, and I found that the movement she made was exactly like that that Kipling described: when the ship goes wop with a wiggle between and the plates begin to slide. . . .

But I did go aboard and there were very brief moments that enchanted me. Too brief to compensate, but well worth remembering.

On one particular day we were out at sea, land only a memory somewhere on the horizon. It was one of the few rare days when the sun shone. On shore people were lying out like meat on a slab, roasting themselves. At sea it was still two-jersey weather, with a wicked little wind riffling the water.

Suddenly over the waves came a tiny bird, so exhausted, it was barely lifting its body above the water. It reached the boat and fluttered up and landed, astounding us, on my husband's pipe stem, close to the bowl, It perched there.

Kym was sunbathing in the cockpit, stretched out lazily, enjoying the fact that this day we did not go up and down with too unseemly a movement, but had a gentle rocking that was extremely irritating but infinitely preferable to the wild rip and roll.

He opened his eyes.

A bird.

On a boat.

On a pipe. In master's mouth.

How absurd.

He plainly didn't believe it, and went to sleep again. The bird flew to our daughter's belt and perched there. It was a tiny greenish bird, which we later identified as a willow warbler, flying goodness knows where. It left the belt and perched on my finger. I was steering.

Then it flew to the compass.

It went into the cabin, and perched on a bunk where it stayed for some considerable time. Recovering, it explored the map, returned to the compass and landed on the seat only a few inches from the cat's face.

He stared at it, still apparently unable to believe his eyes. He probably felt he was dreaming. I was ready to grab him, but he made no move at all, lying lazily in the sun, stretched to his full length which was considerable, while the bird preened itself and ignored the cat completely.

Presently it flew off, refreshed.

Only then did Kym apparently realise it was a bird.

He stood up and watched it go.

'Waugh,' he said, and went back to savour the sunshine, while we headed for shore.

Although I have always been able to do my own thing, and have spent weeks pony trekking, taming a hawk, or animal watching in Ireland, Kenneth, being besotted about the sea, does find it hard to understand how anyone can fail to enjoy it – rather as the mother of a particularly loathsome baby is quite unable to understand that other people may not find his revolting habits in the least charming, or the owner of a totally untrained dog may fail to appreciate that others don't want to be leaped on with muddy paws when dressed in their best clothes, or licked with a tongue that has just savoured something unspeakable.

So when he achieved one of his ambitions and bought *Vayla*, a nine-ton Hillyard, I did promise I would go along and be part of the crew for her maiden voyage from Littlehampton to Anglesey. And of course Kym would come too.

The journey to Littlehampton was rather complicated in that our elder son, by now luckily able to drive, was taking down the rest of us, plus the boat's gear, plus Kym, and we had to arrange for catering long distance.

We arrived in Littlehampton and found the boatyard. *Vayla* unfortunately wasn't quite complete as she lacked a propeller, which somehow had not turned up, whether due to the post or some inability to deliver we didn't know, and neither did Hillyard's, who had built the boat and were very sad indeed that she wasn't ready.

They went to enormous trouble to collect the propeller, driving miles to get it and fitting it, and meanwhile we had to start our holiday in the dock at the boatyard.

This wasn't much of a hardship for me, as there were no waves; no up and down movement, and moreover I could get off the boat whenever I wished and walk on lovely solid dry land.

Well, not very dry, as the tide tended to come over the jetty. Kym didn't like this at all. He said so. Men working on boats beside us (noisily) stared as I lifted my cat over the water. I washed clothes in the paint shed in a small sink, with Kym sitting beside me, investigating a hole that he insisted was a rat hole.

Some minutes later I discovered he was quite right. I wasn't so keen on walking ashore after that. And of course, he was very keen indeed, and at dusk contrived to get himself thoroughly lost among the wood piles, so that we hunted for him endlessly and as soon as we found him, his tail disappeared round another corner. He was most unpopular.

To add to our problems there wasn't any earth for his box and we couldn't use our own lavatory in the dock, but had to walk along the jetty and down a very steep and slippery ladder to a boat that was moored in the tidal part of the boatyard and that belonged to the owner of the yard.

It was a nightmare journey at the best of times; at night it was even worse.

Even boating in a dock had its hazards. One of them, I

knew, would be that I would fall into the sea off the iron rungs, which were atrociously slippery.

At last we put to sea.

There was a brief run with the people from the boatyard aboard, on a voyage to test her out and make sure she was all they said she should be. I had visions of sinking on our maiden voyage, but she behaved very well. We put back, and set off again, inevitably having to wait for the tide to turn. One is always waiting for something in a boat.

Vayla has six berths though to start with there were only three of us aboard, as the boys by now had other lives: one at college, and one in a job. Both were joining us at some point, but our daughter, also at college, had decided to spend the whole month with us. Our older son joined us very shortly, coming across country by train on receipt of a 'phone call.

Meanwhile, the weather decided to favour us with true British unpredictability. It was very rough on the way to the Isle of Wight and by the time we arrived there was a gale warning.

So we had to shelter in port, tied up to dolphins alongside other boats. Not the animals, but wooden posts set in the water. This had hazards too, as Kym, if we didn't watch him, could commute from one boat to another; and people on their way to shore used us as a through road. We had to use other people.

All the boats went up and down together and I retreated to the cabin where I needn't watch the swinging masts. I read. The wind blew. The gale warnings continued. My unfavourite one is at 2 a.m., though 6 a.m. runs it close. One has to listen to them all for safety's sake. We did crossword puzzles, cooked meals, went shopping. At this rate we wouldn't even reach Anglesey but would have to leave the ship in some other place and then work her round later.

I thought of Garnafailagh and the quiet lake and the

sunsets.

We set out for Poole.

It was blustery and Kym and I sat together, while everyone else revelled in the stiff wind, and the cold breeze and wet hands and oilskins. I began to feel that something in my makeup had been missed out, as I was getting more and more bored and with three weeks still to go was extremely tired of grey sea and white wave tops.

Kym shared my boredom. We read books together. He ate and slept and curled up on my lap. I knew he liked being with us, which was some consolation but not much.

There were more gale warnings at Poole, but at last we set out for Brixham. I am never actually sick so get no sympathy whatever. I merely feel very giddy, have a blinding headache and know that if anyone shows me food, or even asks me to cook it, I will jump straight overboard and end my misery.

We went on and on and on and on.

The waves fought us endlessly. The boat slipped down the waves and hauled her horrible self up the waves. Things inside slipped around. The family wanted food. I tried to make sandwiches, knowing that if I did so, I would probably really be sick. The boat hurled herself across a wave top, apparently thinking she was a dancer about to pirouette. Kym fell off one bunk, and I fell off the other, hitting my head on the table, and just for good measure, sitting in the butter, while sliced bread went all over the cabin.

I said things. Kym was saying things too.

We picked ourselves up and I completed the job and crawled into the quarter berth after taking an anti-seasick pill, which is nearly as bad as being sick, as it makes one so sleepy.

I dozed and Kym clung to me, and in between whiles I was aware that the boat was still climbing up the waves and hurling herself down them and everyone else was having a whale of a time.

We reached Brixham.

We anchored in the harbour.

The men went off for diesel fuel and food, while my daughter and I cooked a meal. It was bliss not to be out on the wildly rolling sea. The harbour master drew alongside, his face very angry.

'What do you mean by being here three days and not reporting?' he demanded.

'Three days?' I said. 'We've only been here ten minutes. We've just come in.'

'Are you sure?' he asked.

'Of course I'm sure,' I said, equally furious. 'It's exactly ten minutes since we arrived.'

'I bet it was lumpy outside,' he said. 'The fishing trawlers haven't been out for three days.'

'It was. Very lumpy,' I said.

Kym stuck his head into the cockpit, agreeing wholeheartedly. Everyone laughed.

By now I knew why people went to sea. For the same reason as the madman hit his head constantly against a wall: because it was so nice when he stopped.

Unfortunately we couldn't stay in harbour for ever.

Out we went into the Bristol Channel.

And the wind blew and the rain came, and the waves grew higher and higher.

And this part was even more endless, as not only did it take thirty-six hours, without any chance of avoiding the ceaseless movement, but somewhere in the middle of the night I woke to find the engines had stopped, and were apparently being dismantled, and the two men were arguing wholeheartedly as to what was wrong.

The stars were swinging violently round the sky.

There was nothing I could do so I took my horrible pills, gathered Kym up and went back to sleep.

It was still rough when I woke up. Too rough to make

hot food. Too rough to risk using the cooker, especially as its oven door swung open every time the boat rocked. Too rough to do more than wait and hope that harbour would come soon. By now I had vowed I never would go to sea again. Not even for a so-called day trip, as those are liable to produce hazards such as going aground and missing the tide and having to stay at sea all night, not even prepared for such an eventuality.

That voyage continued rough until we reached the last lap, leading to the Menai Straits.

Kym was sitting on the bench in the cockpit and he saw them first.

'Waugh', he said.

We looked.

There were hundreds of seabirds floating on the waves, basking in the sun, wings outstretched, almost drunk with warmth. There were more than any of us had ever seen in our lives, and as we motored among them, they were so lazy that they barely lifted their wings, flapped away a few yards, and dropped on the water again.

There were eider duck and pochard and teal. There were cormorants and shags and every imaginable kind of gull. There were puffins and there were razor bills. There were terns; and there were birds we had never seen before and could not find in the bird books. The water was covered with them for almost a mile.

And then we were over Caernarvon bar and in the Straits. We would, Kenneth said, spend the last week sun-bathing and fishing and recovering, as even he agreed the going has been tough. Every anchorage we had found for the last few nights had had the wind blowing from the only direction that made it totally unbearable. And the wind changed remorselessly, with unerring accuracy, as soon as we had anchored. In Fishguard, it was totally wrong. At Abersoch, it was unspeakable. At Porth Dinlleyn it had never ever blown from that direction before in all the years they had been boating.

Well, Jonah wasn't going to sea again, that was for sure.

One thing, we were now in home waters, and I could leave the boat in the morning, get on to dry land and sleep in the caravan.

Except of course that you can never make plans on a boat.

While we were waiting for the tide a giant butterfly fell on to the deck. Kym was removed. I gave it two lumps of sugar and watched it use its proboscis to test the food. It then flooded the sugar with saliva which melted it. Six sugar lumps later it spread its wings, revealing itself as a tremendous and beautiful Red Admiral. Later it flew towards the shore. How I envied it.

The weather changed almost as soon as we were over Caernarvon bar.

Straits weather can be atrocious as there is a fast current, and when the wind is one way and the tide is another and against the current the resulting boat movement is quite unspeakable.

The wind blew all day.

There was no chance to leave the boat. We borrowed a mooring at Port Dinorwic, and ate and drank and did crossword puzzles. We were almost out of bread. Anne made a cake.

The wind changed. The weather forecast predicted full scale gales. And we weren't safe.

Kym went to earth in the quarter bunk, where the legs of the sleeper are enclosed in a tunnel. He could endure the rocking there. I tidied up and made everything safe, and husband and daughter worked the boat to just off Lord Anglesey's beautiful home, which is now the Conway training school for officers in the Royal Navy.

One of the masters from the training school yelled at us, as we went to tie up out of the wind.

'You can't moor there, it's private.'

We glared at him. If looks could have killed ours would have killed him, as there were few other places in the Straits where we would be safe for the night. It is narrow and rocky and the wind could blow us ashore.

We motored back to look for shelter elsewhere.

A small fishing boat was moored off Moel y Don, where *Vayla* normally had her moorings. On it were mother and father, and two quite young children. They were in an open boat with only very slight shelter; they were not dressed for the weather, as it was now so cold we were wearing two jerseys each and our oilskins and even so were uncomfortable. They hadn't even jerseys with them. We could not make a hot drink, but they hadn't anything. They had also tied up where the sea and the current were at their worst and the rip of the tide race caught their tiny craft so that conditions for them were utterly unspeakable.

They called to ask if we could help.

We dared not, as we weren't safe ourselves, and any rescue attempt would only have ended in disaster. We couldn't get ashore any more than they could, and if we went near, the tide would fling us against them and they would sink. In fact if they had run their boat aground, they could have got off, but they didn't want to try. It seemed to them better to stay tied up where they were. Conversation was impossible, as by now the noise of the sea and the wind drowned all words.

We motored back down the Straits, past the safety of the Conway training school moorings hating the Conway master wholeheartedly, and finally decided the only thing to do was to anchor off the little heron wood that was on the cliffs about half a mile away from the tubular railway bridge. Any question of going under the bridges did not arise as at the best of times there is an immense swell, called the Swellies, and evil little whirlpools called the Whirlies, and many a boat has come to grief trying to be too bold.

There was nothing to do but sit it out.

Or ride it out.

Husband and daughter went on anchor watch, as I can't balance at the best of times on a boat and I was a considerable hazard when I moved. I fell all over the place, hanging on to the bunks and the table, watching the prow of the boat rise up to the sky and then fall away, so that at one moment I was high in the air, and the next down under the water, with waves rushing green past the portholes.

By now the rest of the crew had fastened themselves by their safety harnesses to the rigging, one holding the tiller to keep the boat into the wind, the other hugging the gypsy so that the anchor didn't drag. I wondered rather idly what my friends would say if I told them I was on the boat all night while my husband cuddled a gypsy.

By now everything was so awful I felt it couldn't really get worse.

The anchor did begin to drag.

I was half way down the quarter berth, with my knees pressed against the sides to keep me from falling all over the place. Kym, occasionally yelling, was anchored firmly inside my anorak, buttoned right up tight. Once he asked to get out and fought his way to his earth box and fell off it and flooded the floor. Nobody cared. He clambered back, walking belly flat against the floor, and I grabbed him, held him to clean himself and then tucked him back again.

The radio was also anchored between my legs, turned full on to distract us from the night.

Cheery voices joked about the weather, and the fact that boats were being tossed at sea and here they were snug in the studio ha ha. Ha ha, we all said bitterly.

Ha ha, Kym said, equally bitterly, telling me he loathed it and why didn't I stop it and what had anyone done to deserve this?

The wind took the trees and tortured them, dragging them down to the beach, their trunks complaining, creaking and groaning. Above the noise of the wind and the anguished screams of the trees sounded the birds, hundreds of voices from the woods, desperately frightened, calling together, an unbelievable cacophony. Heron and pheasant and blackbird; owl and robin and wren; small bird noises, loud bird screams, angry chatterings, on and on, while the waves thundered on the shore and somewhere on the boat a piece of rigging tipped with metal tapped endlessly, maddeningly, and the boat shuddered and shook and sometimes I looked out of the lighted cabin to see my daughter poised high above me, and the next moment I was high above her and her small face looked up at me from a welter of water that seemed to threaten to engulf us any minute.

I had visions of the boat foundering; or being swamped by a giant wave; or overturned; or flung like matchwood to splinter on the vicious rock spikes that I knew lay all along the shore. I wondered if I would be able to swim in all that turmoil and imagined myself emerging from the deep, carrying an equally drowned cat, struggling along the cliffs to the lighted windows where the Conway boys lay safe and snug and where I presumed Lord Anglesey and his family also slept secure, unaware of the hell out there on the water. I hoped that the man who had shouted us away from the comfort of a sheltered mooring was enduring indigestion and nightmares and a very bad conscience, but he was probably also soundly and smugly asleep, feeling he had done his duty in protecting their precious mooring from being contaminated by our vulgar ropes.

The programme changed to hymns and we joined in.

Kym squawked.

The birds shrieked and so did the wind and the water was a white turmoil.

There was a lull, and I stretched myself, and husband and daughter met on deck for a brief conference and then, quite unbelievably, a searchlight swept across us.

There, beyond it, rocking and rolling, was the lifeboat, and a man with a megaphone hailed us.

'Are you all right?'

Ask a silly question.

'Yes', my husband said, lying with all his teeth.

'No', I whispered.

'Waugh', Kym yelled, and we staggered to the doorway of the cabin. We blinked in the searchlight's glare. It can't have been often that the lifeboat men were met by a woman wearing a Siamese cathead that peered from half way up her chest, but nobody seemed perturbed.

'You'd be more comfortable ashore,' they yelled.

I thought of ashore, standing still, not going up and down, and quiet. No slap slap slap of the rigging, no screams from the demented birds, no fear of being flung against the rocks.

'How would we get off?' I asked my husband.

'By a bosun's chair.'

A rope across the water, and the rolling boats, and the cat in my arms. I couldn't face that. OK. We were all right.

'We're going to rescue some people in a little boat at Moel y Don', the voice shouted. 'We'll pass you on the way back. If you want to come off then, we'll take you all ashore.'

The light went out and we watched the boat swing away from us, its small lamps beaming brightly, as it went on its errand. The most wonderful men in the world. Even though we hadn't gone it was good to know they were there and they were coming back.

But by the time they came back, some considerable time later, the lulls were more frequent, the waves were subsiding, the birds had stopped crying and there was a gleam of light along the horizon. No need to come off. They waved to us cheerily and left us. We heard later that the four in the little boat had been in a terrible state, sea-sick and suffering from exposure, not knowing how treacherous weather can be, or that you never ever go out in a boat without taking plenty of spare clothing along. We always have far more warm clothing than we need. And had we not been caught by the lack of decent weather forecasts we would never have been at sea that night.

By four o'clock the wind had died. We boiled water, drank Ribena and whisky, hot, and fell into our bunks and slept until the next evening.

By which time the wind was blowing again, but not so strong.

It was still impossible to get off.

By now we had read every book on the boat. We had done every crossword puzzle on the boat. We were sick of ship's stores and cold food. And we were all heartily tired of the weather.

We went back to Moel y Don and tied up on our own mooring. We tried to lower the rubber dinghy.

It flew.

No chance whatever of going ashore.

Tossing uneasily, we watched the lights go up in Port Dinorwic. We saw the patched lights on the far mountains where people slept safe in their beds, and did not lie, like fools, in a flimsy boat, letting the wind and tides dominate their lives. They had food to eat too, like roast beef and Yorkshire pudding and roast potatoes and peas and fruit and cream. We had the end of the cake and ship's biscuits and couldn't even boil a kettle. I had forgotten what it felt like not to feel sick. That was almost a way of life, like pregnancy. And also I was cramped and stiff from being cooped up and Kym, whenever the boat was still enough to let him, prowled endlessly, as fed up with being cooped up as we were.

We went to bed.

I woke about two in the morning, aware of a thump, thump, thump against our side.

'Waugh,' Kym said.

'We've got burglars,' I said.

Thump. Thump. Thump.

The crew jumped up and we went to look.

The lifeboat had left the abandoned fishing boat moored to a buoy. It hadn't been properly tied up in the first place and had now come adrift and there it was, butting against us, as the tide drove it at us, again and again. It would damage us.

We spent the night sitting up fending it off as it came towards us.

Push away.

Push away.

Push away.

At last the tide turned and we managed to get some sleep, only to wake to a fine sunny morning and see the boat stuck good and hard right in the middle of the fairway. It was now a shipping hazard.

We motored towards it and tried to shift it. We could always claim salvage.

It had its anchor down, and the anchor had fouled something deep under the water. Probably an old mooring. Or a cable.

Nothing would shift it.

And the big oil tankers came to and from Caernarvon to discharge their loads.

'You and Kym can go ashore, walk up to Plas Coch and 'phone the Coastguard about that thing,' my husband said.

That was fine by me. I changed out of the clothes I had spent the gale in, washed, had a hot drink and some breakfast, put on a grey trouser suit and combed my hair and put make-up on. Complete with Kym, I was rowed to the little hard slipway and deposited on dry land.

Dry land was heaven.

We both thought so, and with Kym sitting on my shoulder saying over and over and over, isn't this great, just look at that, just look at me, to everyone who passed, we made a somewhat conspicuous and peculiar progress up the hill to the caravan site. I had the car keys and was to drive down to pick up our gear which had all to come ashore. Few hobbies seem to involve quite so much paraphernalia as sailing.

The hedges were riotous with flowers. The grass had never been so green. The hydrangeas in the gardens of the few houses had never looked so bright. There was colour dazzling me in the trees; there were cattle in the fields and there at last was Plas Coch, and the long drive, past the vans. After a month spent at sea it was like regaining one's sight. I couldn't believe the brilliance, or the way the plants had changed in the time we had spent away.

Kym apparently couldn't believe it either as he grew more and more vocal. He also was remarkably heavy, and though I tried to make him walk, he wasn't having it. He sat, pathetic, poor unsteady cat, not used to being on shore. Couldn't *walk*. So I endured him, nuzzling my ear, yelling at everyone we passed, rousing curious glances. That mad woman and her cat.

I reached the telephone kiosk and went inside.

I hadn't got any money with me. I had a Siamese cat and I had the car keys and the caravan keys and that was it.

And that boat was a considerable danger to shipping and the big tankers came down every day when the weather was fine. There must be a stack of them lying up somewhere.

I went into the telephone kiosk, as there was one thing I could do.

Kym of course came too, and sat on the shelf and watched me dial 999.

Fire, ambulance, police, asked an impersonal voice.

Well, it wasn't the business of the fire brigade and we didn't need an ambulance so that left the police.

'Can I help you,' said a beautiful Welsh voice in deep tones, that made me sure he must sing like an angel.

'There's a boat stuck in the fairway, and it's a danger to shipping,' I said.

Kym leaned forward, fascinated, and said 'Waugh' loud

159

and clear.

'What did you say?' the voice demanded.

'I'm sorry, that was my cat,' I said. And repeated the message. Kym, unable to lean forward as I was holding him back, decided he would shout and then he might be heard too. He produced one of his real noises. A wake-the-dead-and-damn-the-devil noise.

'Are you sure?' the voice said. He must by now be convinced I was completely crazy. I wasn't at all sure that I wasn't.

'Yes. I spent the night pushing it away from our own boat. We got caught in the gale,' I said. Kym corroborated me, fervently. 'I've just got off the boat. We had our cat with us. I thought I'd better ring you as I haven't any money with me.'

It was sounding more and more idiotic, but somehow the penny dropped.

'Quite a gale, wasn't it? I'll phone the harbour master and they'll see to the boat.'

'Waugh,' yelled Kym, to all and sundry.

There was a laugh at the other end.

'Sounds quite a character you've got there.'

I rang off, lifted my character and went to get the car. We unloaded the boat, and came home to eat a meal on dry land, from cups that didn't spill when they were lifted, from plates that didn't slide the food into our laps. We slept.

That night we went out for a meal. Never had food tasted so good.

'We'll have better weather next year,' my husband said, being an incurable optimist.

Next year was a long way away, but it came, in the end, and being a fool, I said well yes, I would try just this once, but if the weather was bad, never again.

We set out at four in the morning, complete with Kym, and our daughter and a schoolfriend of hers.

By half-past four the weather had changed and we had

run into a freak local gale off Llandwyn island. It was only two hours to Holyhead, they said. Twelve sea-sick hours later we arrived at Holyhead, and I put all my clothes in a string bag, much to everyone's horror, and left the boat and the weather and the cat.

I arrived at the caravan not caring if I lived or died, not even caring that I was going to be without Kym at home for three weeks. I lay on the step as my son and his friend were out, and I hadn't a key.

Next door resuscitated me with the biggest brandy I have ever seen. The taxi driver had already treated me like fine porcelain, probably afraid I would die in his car. I wasn't sure I would survive that journey.

I can't recommend feeling simultaneously drunk and sea-sick.

Andrew and his friend came back from a drive round the island, astounded to find me there. I crawled into my bed and lay there, listening unbelievably to the noise of the sea, which shouldn't by any stretch of the imagination have been there at all.

'Can you hear the sea?' I asked them.

Thoughtfully my son listened, then prodded the caravan ceiling with his hand. Twenty-five buckets of water later I discovered I had a new cure for sea-sickness. The rain had been accumulating between the two skins of the roof for years. It took a long time to dry out.

I decided for the first and last time in my life that I would go home to my parents.

There I spent a blissful three weeks of superb weather, lying in the garden in the sun, being thoroughly and deliciously spoilt, as I'd never been able to stay so long before.

The boat crew endured weather as bad as the year before, but being gluttons for punishment, went right on boating, though I gathered the girls had abandoned ship at Arran very briefly and hired bicycles, just to get away from the sea.

I have never been to sea since, and have no intention of doing so, no matter how hard the dedicated try to persuade me I am wrong. I don't mind if they do go to sea; I don't mind what anyone does, so long as I am left to do what I like doing, and not be a pale shadow, trying to pretend I like something I hate. One man's meat is another man's poison, which is probably just as well, as there wouldn't be enough for all.

Kym didn't go to sea again either.

He was now eleven years old, and that is a very good age for a Siamese. He was elderly and slow and a little querulous at times. He had sinusitis frequently as the result of his old dose of cat 'flu and he was getting recurrent attacks of nephritis.

There couldn't be that much longer for Kym.

And then what would I do?

For me, each animal stands on its own, but can never be the last. All I have learned would be wasted, and what I have learned enables me to give another animal a better life; to avoid some mistakes. No other cat would go to kennels without far more inspection, just for a start. That had left too long a legacy.

But that was in the future.

There was still time left to us.

And I valued every minute.

Chapter 13

The sun became important to Kym. He had rheumatism in his leg, and often when he stood would draw in his breath a little, gasping, like an old man saying 'oof' as he feels a twinge in an old injury. Kym followed the sun round the house.

He still wandered, but I found his wanderings were very curtailed as when my neighbour and I compared notes we discovered he went out at eight and arrived at her house at eight fifteen, where he spent his time till dinner time, when he would come back home. He went back to her as soon as he was let out, as her bedroom was sunnier than mine.

He left her about four and was home by four fifteen.

Often he spent the day lying in the sun under the veronica bush; or under the winter jasmine, or curled in the heather at the bottom of the garden.

He no longer travelled very far away from the house and he no longer fought every other cat. He avoided fights, and at least we were spared those endless trips to the vet for treatment for abscesses. Now instead we needed to watch his kidneys and his sinusitis, which both could be controlled. I took him to the vet at the first sign of illhealth as that meant one treatment instead of three.

By now too I was getting busier with my writing, and so the vet came to me more often than not. Kym knew him and accepted treatment, never jibbing at an injection, though sometimes he behaved like a kitten when I had to give him pills.

Then it was necessary to chase him, and grab him and wrap him in a towel and force open his mouth, push the pill to the back of his throat and stroke him to make him swallow.

Also at this time he evolved a new game, as he seemed to perk up at night. He decided he would not go to bed anywhere but with me. We decided as he was now a noisy sleeper, and snored, that he would go right on sleeping where he always slept at home and that was in his basket in the kitchen, which had the virtue that in winter it was very warm.

He always greeted me so fervently in the morning that breakfast was often late.

Now he raced upstairs at bedtime and under a bed. Try and get him and he ran around the other side, always just out of reach, always watching us with a wicked expression, knowing we were getting mad as he usually waited until we were extremely tired before carrying out this exercise. He possibly thought in his funny cat mind that one day we would relent and let him stay, but in the end we always won, one of us on one side of the bed, one on the other, trapping him and carrying him down, where he shouted piteously until at last he decided that wasn't doing much good.

He could still jump and it was still necessary to move cream and the milkjug very fast, or that inquisitive paw would dip in and be sucked.

He was so very slow, otherwise.

One morning, when he was almost twelve years old, Beagle came round. It must have been a new beagle as he was still full of puppy vigour. He chased Kym, who ran into our neighbour's garden. She chased Beagle off and rang me, as Kym had vanished and she was afraid he might have had a heart attack and be lying somewhere in her garden.

I had a friend in to coffee that day and the family were at home.

We searched.

Under the blackcurrants and the rhubarb. In the shed

and in the house. In the shrubbery and among the flowers that grew tall in the herbaceous border. In our own garden.

Animals creep away to die in peace. I was sure Kym had done just this and gone to the fields opposite where a friend's Scottie had chosen to die a few years before. There would be no finding him except by accident, as we had found poor Kirstie. By then it was too late.

We gave up and sat drinking coffee, not very happily, not saying very much.

Suddenly I heard a soft 'Waugh', and looked out of the window.

There in the apple tree, his eyes bright with wickedness, sat my cat. He had probably been there all the time, watching us, listening to us, not choosing to come, possibly entertained by our idiocy.

He came down very carefully, and jumped into my lap, purring.

He came away just once more to Anglesey where he spent most of the time asleep, not wandering far, and had to go to the vet as the grass was seeding and his sinuses were bad again.

At home he spent almost every minute of the day now beside me, either by my typewriter, or in my lap. He had ceased visiting, as my neighbour had moved. The vet had promised to tell me when the moment came, when I would be keeping him alive for my own selfishness.

But it hadn't come yet.

Christmas came and went, and Kym enjoyed every minute, rustling through paper as he had done when very small; sleeping in any cardboard box that we left for him but absenting himself more often from strangers, coming back only when the family were there.

He was very ill in February but he recovered.

Then came Easter.

We were due to go to the caravan: Kenneth to paint the boat, and I to relax after finishing a book. Kym wasn't well enough to travel, but our daughter had exams coming and wanted to stay at home and work and she was every bit as good a nurse as I.

We left them.

I rang home on the Easter Monday and was told that Kym was very ill indeed. But the vet wouldn't put him to sleep without my permission.

And I wouldn't give it, as Kym was going to die in my arms and nowhere else. We went home next day, saying very little. Kym was lying on the chair in our daughter's bedroom when I got home. He greeted me, purring and rubbing his head against me. He was now very plump, which puzzled me as he ate so little. My vet wanted him dieted and I suspect did not believe me when I said the cat scarcely ate anything.

Kym spent the night beside me.

In the morning I rang the vet.

'You know what I have to say,' he said.

'Yes. And please get it over, quick.'

He promised to come early. I put Kym in the sunshine that dappled the floor, and quite suddenly he grabbed my hand with his two front paws and nuzzled it. He rolled and stretched and purred, rubbing against me, on and on, endlessly, over and over, as if he were saying how much he had liked us and being with us, as if he knew that this was the end.

An hour later, he was dead. He had not been afraid, right up to the last, only very angry, when his paw was shaved so that the vet could find the vein.

I had an autopsy done as I wanted to know why he had died, and also felt it might help to save another cat later if we knew what had been wrong. He hadn't been fat at all. His kidneys had been failing through cancer and he had dropsy. The vet apologised for his disbelief. He had actually been a very thin cat, and if that wretched fluid hadn't masked his gauntness we might have guessed how ill he was.

But I was assured that he hadn't suffered. The pain would have started in a day or so. And he had had a long and full life and enjoyed every minute of it, right up to his last illness.

The house was dead.

No purring cat to greet us. No raucous shout of anger or dismay or amusement as he appeared. We burned all his possessions, Viking-like, unable to face them.

We went indoors, but there was nothing for us there. Only Anne and I were at home. We went out, had a meal out, went shopping and came in to get a meal no one wanted at all.

That night I dreamed I was in a wood and Kym was running away from me. His cries grew fainter and fainter as I ran calling, calling, calling. Then they stopped and I woke, knowing this time the dream was true and no amount of calling could bring him back.

I went down into the silent kitchen.

It was time for Anne to go back to college. After she had gone, and the men had gone to work, the house was very still. Uncannily still. I looked into the garden and there under the veronica bush, I saw Kym. I stared. He didn't move.

Unbelieving, I went into the garden. There couldn't be a cat there. But there was.

Next door's black cat stared up at me, safely ensconced in Kym's favourite place. I looked at the heather bed and there was a tabby cat I had never seen before in my life. A ginger cat crouched on the fence. Another black cat was under the winter jasmine.

There were cats everywhere I looked. Eight of them, watching me, in an uncanny silence. Four I knew. They had all been Kym's enemies, warned off his territory. Now they were staking claims. Or were they mourning?

I didn't know. I remembered how Kym had gone across

the road when Sandy died.

I knew I couldn't stand the silent house and haunted garden and I went out, to nowhere, to wander round the shops, not wanting to come home to a house where nothing moved except myself.

Next day I rang the vet.

'Kym was a wonderful cat', he said. He told me the result of the post mortem. He knew how I felt. Only a cat, but he had been a major part of my life for thirteen years, with me more often than any member of my family, beside me when I wrote, travelling with me, lying against me, sharing so many experiences that led in the end to one or another of my books.

He had been dead for only two days and both were pointless and endless. I didn't care if all the carpets were ripped and all the paper torn off the walls. Just so long as there was a small live thing to rush and greet me when I came home, and to teach as I had taught Kym, to come around with us.

'Where can I get another Siamese cat?' I asked the vet.

'I don't know', he said. 'But you've always hankered for a dog. You wouldn't have one with Kym around. I know where there is a golden retriever pup. Why don't you get one?'

I hadn't thought of a dog.

I hated being without one and had begged and borrowed one for years. My latest, Brandy, a yellow Labrador, I had just abandoned, as his owner seemed to come second best in Brandy's affections and it wasn't fair to keep taking him out and alienating him from the people who cared about him. I had walked him when Kym got too old to come places with me and needed to rest, as his owners had a business and no time to exercise the dog.

I went out and bought my pup.

I did all the wrong things and bought him in a hurry to replace a gap I couldn't bear. And he in his turn proved to be a major character, and a major headache.

Within a month I had heard of a litter of Siamese; three seal points and two blue points. I visited and discovered that the blue points were named after characters in my favourite book, *The Lord of the Rings*. Numenor Elrond and Numenor Celeborn. The king and queen of the fairies, two delicious elves who came to me, of their own free will. I couldn't decide on either and bought them both. Their pet names are Chia and Casey, after the cats in two of my books.

Then later came my Alsatian bitch, and her puppies.

We have a houseful now, and I have plans for more when we move to our new cottage with its two acres of land. There will always be animals in my home. I can't imagine life without them. They are part of me, and they are the basis for my writing.

But somehow, I cannot imagine that there will ever be another cat like Kym.

Noisy, obstinate, obstreperous, wilful, demanding, making his presence known to everyone, overcoming all obstacles to achieve his desires, ignoring disability, giving us years of fascination.

His voice haunts me still, full of wonder, as he finds yet another surprise to fascinate him in a world that must be permanently far beyond a cat's understanding.

Waugh!

My two little cats have echoes of him; moments when they trigger memory, but somehow, they don't seem to measure up.

He was quite a cat.

None of us will ever forget him.

BREED OF GIANTS
By JOYCE STRANGER

Few of those who have seen the Shire Personality of the Year, standing splendid in the spotlight at the Horse of the Year Show, dwarfing the herald's more delicate mounts, will ever forget the giant horse—proud and handsome, head held high, mane brilliant with tiny standards, tail braided with ribbons.

This book tells the story of Josh Johnson, a farmer, who breeds his gigantic Shire horses and, with fanatical devotion, brings them up to championship status, only to have his hopes shattered by an accident to his best horse and an outbreak of foot-and-mouth disease on a neighbouring farm.

How Josh copes with his burdens and builds once more his winning strain of Shires, is told with all Joyce Stranger's skill and charm.

0 552 09893 0—**85p**

ZARA
By JOYCE STRANGER

'Starting with a detailed description of the golden-brown racehorse, Zara, Mrs Stranger traces a stage in the development of a family, the Prouds, who run the stud where Zara is stabled and trained. She shows Richard Proud's obsession with horses, a passion complete to the extent that it sometimes causes unjustifiable neglect of Zara's chief rival, his wife Stella.

Against a background of family misunderstanding, friction and ill-health, Mrs Stranger balances the excitement of racing in Yorkshire with all the trials and tribulations of winter snow storms and isolation.'

Oldham Evening Chronicle

0 552 09892 2—**80p**

RUSTY

By JOYCE STRANGER

A powerful and impressive story. Joyce Stranger is absolutely honest with her characters, and they are all the more attractive for such treatment . . . Rusty himself is no semi-human pet, but a real stag with dangerous habits and barely suppressed instincts . . .

The story is full of excitement, and though, like any honest animal story from *Black Beauty* onwards, it is bound to be tragic, there is also plenty of humour and the ending is full of hope.

0 552 10126 5—**75p**

NEVER TELL A SECRET

By JOYCE STRANGER

Life at Shallow Dene Farm had never been easy, but 12-year-old Shanie was used to helping her father and caring for the animals. Somehow, they managed to get by. Then suddenly, in one terrible afternoon, the peace of the little farm was shattered: vandals from then earby town arrived on motorbikes and as well as stealing from the house, they killed and injured many of the animals.

Shanie was heartbroken, but as the weeks went on, she discovered that one of the cats who had lost her kittens in the raid had made a home in an old haunted house, and had adopted two orphans—a kitten . . . and a fox cub. Shanie decided that the little family needed protecting— and she was determined to keep this secret to herself . . .

0 552 10397 7—**85p**

CASEY

By JOYCE STRANGER

The touching story of a cat with a difference.

Life at Wayman's Corner could never be dull. Crises lurked around every corner ... marital friction, careless city visitors, farmyard accidents, and Casey.

Casey, son of a Siamese tomcat and a black farmcat, was an animal with great determination, strong affections, and a nose for mischief, whose strange friendship with Sultan the terrifying Jersey bull, becomes a central part of life on the farm ...

0 552 10125 7—**85p**

CHIA THE WILDCAT

By JOYCE STRANGER

Chia!

—the sound of the wildcat—as explosive as a gun-shot, as sharp as a slash of claws ...

No tame and gentle fireside tabby, Chia is a prowling savage beast, who comes out of the night to kill. Often the only traces of her presence are stray feathers, blood-spattered bones and her terrifying wails in the night.

The wildcat has no friends but many enemies—the most feared of which is man. So Chia makes her home far from human haunts, where the looming shadow and the lethal gun of the hunter will not menace her kittens.

But even there the eagle and the fox give her no rest ... and the wild cry rings out over the rolling glens—

Chia!

0 552 09891 4—**70p**

LOVE IN THE DOG HOUSE
By MOLLY DOUGLAS

Molly and Christopher Douglas discovered that everything could and did happen when they began to breed and board dogs on their Manitoba farm.

There were cockers, beagles, chihuahuas and Assorted others . . . all kept in order by the Major, an elderly beagle of military bearing who kept strict discipline in the doggy ranks. There was Star, the toy terrier, who bullied the bull, and Twan Fu, the shih tzu, who arrived on a silver leash with day and night blankets, brush, comb, raincoat and choco drops, and had the time of his life rolling in cow pats and living like a real dog.

There were the people who came to buy and board, and dogs who were supposed to mate—and wouldn't. And above all there was the Douglas family, who turned their home into

THE DOG HOUSE . . .

0 552 11333 6—**85p**

JUDITH
By ARITHA VAN HERK

Winner of the Seal $50,000 Canadian First Novel Award.

Judith the unanimous and enthusiastic choice of a panel of literary experts in London, New York and Toronto. A novel of rare power and refreshing originality—utterly unforgettable.

There were two Judiths: the elegant city secretary trapped in a sordid affaire with her boss—and the little country girl she'd once been, who knew as much about hog-raising as her Dad. And when Dad died, so did city Judith. The bitter girl who abandoned her life and returned to her roots, was a loner, and intended to stay that way. A force to be reckoned with who can take on a pig farm single-handed— or a bar room full of angry men . . . And when a man came along who could re-awake her passion, Judith was not ready to give up her independence . . .

0 552 11192 9—**95p**

CATHERINE COOKSON NOVELS
IN CORGI

WHILE EVERY EFFORT IS MADE TO KEEP PRICES LOW, IT IS SOMETIMES NECESSARY TO INCREASE PRICES AT SHORT NOTICE. CORGI BOOKS RESERVE THE RIGHT TO SHOW AND CHARGE NEW RETAIL PRICES ON COVERS WHICH MAY DIFFER FROM THOSE ADVERTISED IN THE TEXT OR ELSEWHERE.

THE PRICES SHEWN BELOW WERE CORRECT AT THE TIME OF GOING TO PRESS (MAY 80)

☐ 11160 0	THE CINDER PATH	£1.25
☐ 10916 9	THE GIRL	£1.50
☐ 11202 X	THE TIDE OF LIFE	£1.50
☐ 11374 3	THE GAMBLING MAN	£1.25
☐ 11204 6	FANNY MCBRIDE	95p
☐ 11261 5	THE INVISIBLE CORD	£1.25
☐ 11087 6	THE MALLEN LITTER	£1.25
☐ 11086 8	THE MALLEN GIRL	£1.25
☐ 11085 X	THE MALLEN STREAK	£1.25
☐ 09894 9	ROONEY	95p
☐ 11391 3	PURE AS THE LILY	£1.25
☐ 09373 4	OUR KATE	£1.00
☐ 09318 1	FEATHERS IN THE FIRE	£1.25
☐ 11203 8	THE DWELLING PLACE	£1.25
☐ 11260 7	THE INVITATION	95p
☐ 11365 4	THE NICE BLOKE	95p
☐ 08849 8	THE GLASS VIRGIN	£1.25
☐ 11360 2	THE BLIND MILLER	£1.00
☐ 11434 0	THE MENAGERIE	£1.00
☐ 11367 0	COLOUR BLIND	£1.00
☐ 11448 0	THE UNBAITED TRAP	£1.00
☐ 11335 2	KATIE MULHOLLAND	£1.50
☐ 11447 2	THE LONG CORRIDOR	95p
☐ 11449 9	MAGGIE ROWAN	£1.25

All these books are available at your bookshop or newsagent, or can be ordered direct from the publisher. Just tick the titles you want and fill in the form below.

CORGI BOOKS, Cash Sales Department, P.O. Box 11 Falmouth, Cornwall. Please send cheque or postal order, no currency.

U.K. Please allow 30p for the first book, 15p for the second book and 12p for each additional book ordered to a maximum charge of £1.29.

B.F.P.O. & EIRE allow 30p for the first book, 15p for the second book plus 12p per copy for the next 7 books, thereafter 6p per book.

Overseas customers. Please allow 50p for the first book plus 15p per copy for each additional book.

Name (block letters) ....

ADDRESS ....

(MAY 80) ....